The
Big Red
of C

Kevin Sullivan

SIGMA PRESS

Reprinted 1985, 1987, 1988

ISBN: 0 905104 68 4

Typesetting and Production by:

DESIGNED PUBLICATIONS LTD
8-10 Trafford Road
Alderly Edge
Cheshire

Published by:

SIGMA PRESS
5 Alton Road
Wilmslow
Cheshire SK9 5DY

Distributed by:

JOHN WILEY AND SONS LTD
Baffins Lane
Chichester Sussex PO19 1UD
United Kingdom

Printed and bound in Great Britain by
J. W. Arrowsmith Ltd., Bristol

Preface

C is fast becoming one of the most popular programming languages. It is being used to write everything from operating systems through to spreadsheet calculators and database management systems. Its popularity stems from two distinct advantages. Firstly it is a very flexible language. It is equally at home being used for routine applications such as data retrieval from files and for more 'low level' applications like printer drivers. Secondly any programs written in it are automatically very transportable. No language can claim 100% standardisation, and C is no exception, but it does approach that elusive claim. With little or no modification programs written in one C compiler will be able to be run on most other C compilers.

This book takes the programmer, new to C, through most of the more directly useful commands and statements. It does not claim to be a 'comprehensive' treatment of the language, but simply aims to provide the novice C programmer with a thorough grounding in the majority of the language and some of its more useful applications. It may also help other programmers to get some idea of the types of problems that C is ideally suited to solving, and those that it is not.

A number of people have assisted in a wide variety of ways in the preparation and planning of this book. In particular I would like to thank the following:-
Earl C Terwilliger, Larry Richards, Tom Sellers, Frank Shannon and Eric Meyer, of the LC users's group for providing information and some of the more sophisticated source codes used in the later chapters. Cliff Musson of CUMANA Ltd for providing the 'Hard disk drive' used in much of the filing and sort routines. Dave Lathan, Nick Cardwell and Arie Kiselstein of Silicon Valley Computer Center for their efficient and helpful service and continued support.

Two other textbooks are referred to in this text. These are "Software Tools in Pascal" by B. Kernighan and P. Plauger and "The C programming language" by B. Kernighan and D. Ritchie. They are published by Addison-Wesley and Prentice-Hall respectively. Some of the ideas and programs mentioned throughout this text are developed further by both of these books.

CP/M © Digital Research,
Box 579, Pacific Grove, California.

DeSmet C © C Ware Corp,
1607 New Brunswick Ave,
Sunnyvale California.

LC © Jim Frimmel Misosys,
P.O. Box 4848, Alexandria Virginia.

UNIX © Bell Labs.

LDOS © Logical Systems Inc.,
11520 N. Port Washington Road,
Mequon WI 53092.

Contents

Pointers to structures.
Arrays of structures.
Structures of structures.

Theory behind the Shell sort.
Internal and external sorting.
One method of internal sorting.
One method of external sorting.

Chapter 1

An Introduction to C

The language C was developed at Bell Laboratories in 1972. It was created by Dennis Ritchie and was based on another computer language called B which was itself a development of BCPL (basic combined programming language). It seemed logical that the language that followed B should be C. One of the main strengths of C is that it is a very small language, in terms of the amount of syntax that it has. It is, however, very flexible and can easily be extended to include any number of additional features that the programmer wishes.

Closely associated with C is the operating system called UNIX, which was originally implemented on certain hardware systems. As the job of maintaining and transporting it to other computer configurations was becoming more and more difficult, the systems designers looked for a more flexible language to use when writing the operating system. C was ideal for this purpose, since the language could be produced by a very small amount of processor dependent code, after which the operating system could be written in C itself. This arrangement meant that the time taken to transport UNIX from one machine to another was considerably reduced. It follows that for many people the association of UNIX and C is an extremely close one. In this book we will be basing our programs on two C compilers. These are available for the PC-DOS and MS-DOS LDOS and CP/M 80 or CP/M 86 operating systems. They are both slightly smaller than standard implementations of the full C language, but the differences are minor. The advantage is that any of the programs entered here will be able to run on almost every other computer that supports a C package.

C is a compiled language. This means that any program is first written in a source code or high level language, which is then converted by the computer into the object code or low level language that the computer uses. In our two systems the object code is produced and the program is checked for errors. This object code is then linked or bound with some standard code modules to produce the final code. Some systems can use many more stages in their compilation. These tend to be slower in the compilation stage but often have somewhat more flexible features in the language itself.

We have said that the language is flexible, this is because any program is composed of functions which can be added to and modified quite easily. The effect of this is to produce an easily extensible language, with particularly useful functions (or even complete programs) being stored on disk for use by other programs.

The first program example that we will look at is called program 1 and it simply demonstrates one or two of the more fundamental points about a C program.

```
/*......program 1 the smallest C program......*/

main()
{
}
```

The program begins with a comment line telling us that the program is called program 1 and that it is the smallest C program. Strictly speaking this is not true, since if we were to remove the comment line the program would be shorter. However the important part of the program is what follows the comment line. Each comment line starts with the characters /* and ends with */. They may appear anywhere in a program and since there are no line numbers to act as references we will use comment lines in our discussions of the initial programs.

The program consists of a single function called main(). Every program has to have this function name in if it is to compile properly. The position of main() in the program is unimportant but it must be present somewhere. The point of the brackets will be explained later in the book. The braces following the function name will be used to enclose the code lines of the program. For the time being there are no code lines and so the program will do nothing, as we saw earlier this is the simplest C program possible. The braces mark the beginning and end of each function. If one or other of them are missed out then the program will not compile properly.

The braces may be put in the program in another way, this is shown below.

```
main() {}
```

The main problem with this layout is that in a proper program the code lines tend to become very confusing and difficult to understand. For this reason we will always use the first of the two layouts in our programs.

Summary So Far.

We have seen the use of comment lines and functions. The following are all acceptable comments:

```
/* another comment */
/* main calculation section */
/* opens the file EMPLOYEE/DAT */
```

The following are all acceptable function names:

first()
average()
filecreate()

Each function consists of a function name and then the code. This code starts and ends with braces, which are essential. There is only one compulsory function, called main(), which must be present somewhere in the program.

Our next program example illustrates the way in which the program can be extended by the use of function calls. Here our first function is called main() and the function that is called is callit(). As before the two functions do nothing at all, they are purely to illustrate the techniques.

```
/*......program 2 the smallest C program with a function call.......*/

main()
{
        callit();
}
/*...callit is a dummy function it does nothing...*/

callit()
{
}
```

Program 2 starts with a comment line. The function main() starts with the opening brace and has one command. This calls the function callit() and the command is terminated by a semi-colon. Every separate C command must end with a semi-colon. When the program is executed the code contained in the function callit() would be carried out at this point.

Any function called in a program must exist somewhere in the program. Function callit() follows function main() and simply consists of the function name followed by the pair of braces. As we said earlier, this program also does nothing, it is only to illustrate the use of function calls.

There is rather more to function calls than this but for the moment we will restrict ourselves to looking on functions as ways of executing a defined piece of code e from within another function.

Program example 3 introduces the technique of printing a message onto the screen. This is a standard technique and will be used continually throughout our programs.

```
/*....program 3 screen printing in C....*/

main()
{
        printf("hello out there\n");
}
```

Program 3 starts with the comment line that acts as a title to the program. The function main() is the only one that is present and contains a single command. This is printf() which is the standard screen output command. Inside the brackets of printf(), any characters that are to be printed are placed between quote marks. In our example the message 'hello out there' would be printed onto the screen. C outputs in a stream fashion, which means that successive uses of the printf() command would result in each set of characters appearing next to each other. The language does not add line feeds automatically. In other words if we wanted to add a line feed we have to express this explicitly. In our example program 3 this is done by the use of the\n command. Whenever this appears in a string of characters a line feed will be sent through to the screen. Normally the \n command will be placed at the end of the message, or string that is to be printed. Once again we see that the command is terminated by a semi-colon and the function begins and ends with a pair of braces.

Program 4 introduces another screen formatting command,\t which simply tabs the cursor position on the screen. The normal tab positions are every eight positions, but this may vary from machine to machine.

```
/*....program 4 more detailed screen printing....*/

main()
{
        printf(" \tThis is Kevin Sullivan saying HELLO\n");
}
```

Apart from this one minor difference, and the different message, the two programs are identical. The principle of stream output can be seen from the following program.

```
/*....program 5 an alternative to program 4....*/

main()
{
        printf("this");
        printf(" ");
        printf("is");
        printf("Kevin");
        printf(" ");
        printf("Sullivan");
        printf(" ");
        printf("saying");
        printf(" ");
        printf("HELLO");
        printf(" \n");          /* this is the one that produces the line feed */
}
```

Program 5 has eleven commands within main(). These are all printf() commands and are all terminated by the use of a semi-colon. Each will print a set of characters on the screen, as defined by the text within the quotes. Since there is no line feed command until the last printf() the text will all be printed on the same line. The command that does cause a line feed is indicated by a comment.

The last example program that we will look at in this chapter is one to output a variable to the screen. This is, of course, an essential part of almost any program and we will introduce the concept of assignment of variables in C.

```
/*....program 6 output of variables in C....*/

main()
{
        int length;

        length = 100;
        printf("the size of the book so far is %d pages.\n ",length);
}
```

Program 6 starts, as ever, with a comment line and also has only one function main(). There are three command lines in the function, each ending with a semi-colon. The first command 'int' states that the variable name 'length' represents an integer quantity.

The line length = 100; assigns the value 100 to variable length. It is vitally important that the assignment operator = is not confused with the equality operator ==, which can easily happen.

The final line in the function is printf("the size of the book so far is %d pages.\n",length); This prints out the message as before and also the value represented by length. The characters %d indicate the position in the text where the value of length is to be placed and the fact that it is an integer quantity. Whenever an integer is to be placed in an output line the characters %d are used. Multiple integers can be output, as in the example below:

```
        printf("another example %d and %d and even %d\n",first,second,third);
```

Here the value of first would be placed at the first occurrence of %d, the value of second would be placed at the second %d and the value of third would be placed at the final occurrence of %d.

In this way relatively complex data presentations can be produced on screen with all accompanying messages.

Summary of Chapter 1.

(1)   Comment lines start with /* and end with */.

(2)   Every program has to have at least one function, called main().

(3)   The program code within a function must start and end with the relevant braces e.g. {}.

(4)   Each statement of a function must end with a semi-colon i.e printf(); .

(5)   The screen print commands \n and \t are used to generate a line feed and a tabulation respectively.

(6)   The command printf() is used to output text and variables to the screen. Text must be within quote marks and integer variables are positioned within the text by the use of the %d characters. Multiple variables can be output in this way.

Chapter 2

Control Loops in C

Structured Programming

In all computer languages sections of code are repeated and choices have to be made with regards to the flow of control within a program. This can get out of hand, particularly with the older languages, and especially if excessive use is made of the unconditional GO TO statement. Many of the modern computer languages are so formed that the programmer is forced into using other techniques to transfer control within a program. C is no exception to this and a large number of control statements are provided for.

The essential aim of a well structured program is that it should be relatively easy to maintain and to understand. In writing a 'structured' program the programmer has to bear in mind three guiding principles:

(1)   The overall flow of the program should be sequential.
      There should be no jumping backwards and forwards from one section of code to another.

(2)   Any sections of code that are repeatedly executed should be used in an iterative way. This means that they should be written out once and repeated from within a loop.

(3)   All transfer of control should be done explicitly by the use of IF...THEN....ELSE constructs or the logical equivalent.

All of these guidelines will be used throughout this book. In fact C is so written that it is very difficult to write a successful program without using them. Unfortunately C lends itself to the production of highly 'structured' pieces of code. Frequently these take the form of three or more expressions contained within a single expression, instead of being written out as a number of single lines of code. While these expressions are impressive examples of complex logic they only serve to make the programs almost unreadable. Their only advantage is that they can save a little memory space. The overriding aim of this book is to produce easy to understand examples of the C language, and therefore these types of expression will not be used.

At the end of this section we will look at some of the commands and their flowcharts.

The IF.....ELSE Statement.

This is one of the simplest control statements in C, and as such it appears frequently in many of our programs. We will illustrate it in a formal way and then give a simple example of its use in a short program.

EX1   if (expression) statement1

EX2   if (expression) statement1
       else statement2

In both of these cases statement1 is carried out if the result of the (expression) is found to be true. In EX1 the following program line is executed if the expression in brackets is found to be false. In EX2 the else command forces an explicit transfer of control if the expression is found to be false. The contents of (expression) can be any acceptable C expression.

Unfortunately, we are unable to introduce the use of the if...else construct without using another C command. This is the getchar() command, and it is used to get a character from the keyboard. Its use is very similar to BASIC's INKEY$ command. However it can be used for either digits or characters.

```
/*    program 7 an introduction to if...else */

main()

{

        int reply;

        printf("are you happy with the book ?\n ");    /*line 2*/
        printf("please type <y> for yes or <n> for no.\n ");
/*line 3*/


        reply = getchar();   /*line 4*/
        if (reply == 'y')   /*line 5*/
                printf("well i am very pleased to hear that\n ");
/*line 6*/
        else
                printf("sorry about that have you tried history
instead\n ");   /*line 7*/
}
```

Program 7 starts with a comment line and consists of one function main(). The variable reply is defined as an integer by the int reply; statement. Lines 2 and 3 print out the message in the same way that we saw in chapter 1. Line 4 gets the user's response from the keyboard and assigns its value to the variable, reply. The command getchar() returns an integer value, that is why it was necessary to define reply as being an integer.

The first part of the if....else command is shown in line 5. Here reply is tested to see if it is equal to the character 'y'. We have to enclose y in single quote marks because reply is an integer value and we are comparing it with a character. By using single quotes the compiler will convert the character 'y' into its numeric form. This will vary from compiler to compiler, depending on the processor in use, but normally this numeric value will be the ASCII value of the character. If reply is found to be equal to 'y' then the statement in line 6 will be executed. The else command means that line 7 will be carried out if the test fails (if reply is equal to any other value).

The command (reply == 'y') is what we referred to as an expression in our formal definition of the if.....else statement.
The double equals sign is used to test for equality as distinct from the single equals sign which means "is given the value of". The difference can be seen from the following examples:-

(1)	test = a;
(2)	bill = fred;
(3)	a = average;
(4)	d == result;
(5)	pay == notalot;
(6)	c == funtolearn;

In the examples 1-3 the variable on the left is given the value of the variable on the right. So in the case of (2) if fred was equal to 99 and bill was equal to 1098 before the statement, they would both be equal to 99 after the statement was executed.

Examples 4-6 are all examples of equality statements. As such they are meaningless since they are taken "out of context", but in the correct statements the variable on the left would be compared with the one on the right to test if they were equal.

We can now go on to look at a rather more sophisticated example of the if......else command.

d/* program 8 nested ifs and function calls */

#include stdio/csh;

main()

{

```
          int reply;

          message();

          reply = getchar();
          if (reply == 1)
              bighead();
            else if(reply == 2)
                modest();
          else if(reply == 3)
              assist();


}
message()
{
          printf("hello would you consider yourself \n ");
          printf("brilliant._____ type <1> \n ");
          printf("average._____ type <2> \n ");
          printf("rather below normal._____ type <3>\n ");
          printf(" \n \n ");
          printf("your answer please\n ");
          printf("\n \n \n ");
}

bighead()
{
          printf("!!! well you modest person you, is it possible to get hats to fit your
size head?? \n ");
}

modest()
{
          printf("its pleasant to meet someone as unassuming as yourself \n");
}

assist()
{
          printf("dont give up just because you are having difficulty with this
book.\n");
          printf("you could always try history you know!.\n");
}
```

Program number 8 shows how the if.....else command can be used to produce a
range of possible control branches. The variable used to store the key response is
'reply' (we will look at variables in more detail in chapter 3), and is declared in the
first line of the function main. This program also has a new command at the start.
This is the #include stdio/csh; line which makes the compiler include various
definitions in with the main program.

This could have been omitted but in later programs we will have to make the required definitions explicitly if this module is left out. The type of definitions that are covered by this are definitions of EOF (end of file) and EOL (end of line). Different computers have quite different codes for these and other standard markers. By using a pre-defined external routine (like stdio/csh) these hardware dependent features can be left out of the language proper.

The CP/M compiler will use a slightly different form of declaring the #include stdio/csh module. In general to convert from the LDOS compiler we would replace the #include stdio/csh command by #include cstdio.csh . All the various options that can be included in any program will be dealt with in a later section of the book.

After the definition of the variable reply as an integer the function message() is carried out. This prints four text lines, then two blank lines followed by another text line, then three final blank lines. The text lines prompt the user to press a key selecting whatever attribute they consider applicable!

The reply = getchar() statement assigns the value of whatever key is pressed to the variable reply. This is then tested by the three if.....else statements that follow. These should be reasonably self explanatory, with the relevant function being called if the corresponding test is found to be true. If the key pressed does not correspond to one of the tests then the program terminates at the end of the tests. Once any of the messages has been printed the program will terminate.

The WHILE statement.

The if.....else statement is very useful but there are a number of applications where it would be neater for us to have a different means of testing a particular condition. If we wanted some section of a program to be carried out until a particular condition was met it would be far easier to use the while..... statement. The formal construction is shown below.

    while (expression) statement;

Once again the semi-colon is required. The formal syntax shows that while the test contained in 'expression' is interpreted as true then whatever commands are in 'statement' will be carried out. The test for 'expression' is done at the start of the while..... statement and so if the test is false the statement lines are not carried out. Only simple examples will be given since we will look at a complete working program later on.

```
/* program 8 an introduction to while... */

main()

{
int a;
a = 1;
while(a <= 10)
```

```
        {
        printf("this is an example of a while condition\n  ");
        a = a + 1;
        }
}
```

Here we have a single function called main(). In it a variable 'a' is declared as being an integer, and is assigned a value of 1 by means of the a = 1; statement. The remainder of the program is devoted to the while..... loop. The expression part of the loop is (a <= 10) and the statement that follows is everything within the pair of braces. REMEMBER: C uses braces to delimit (divide up) sections of program. In our formal syntax of the while..... statement we said that only one statement would follow the expression. Strictly speaking this is so, but by making that statement start and end with braces we can include any number of commands in it.

So in our simple example 'a' is tested and if it is less than or equal to 10 the two statement lines following are carried out. These simply print out a message and then add one to the value of 'a'. This test is carried out each time that the loop is executed and eventually the test value is exceeded and the program terminates. (We have used a method of incrementing 'a' that would be common in many other computer languages ie a = a + 1. C allows us to use a much more efficient method which we will look at later in the book.)

There is a version of the while..... command called the do.... while statement which is identical to the example just given except for the fact that the body of the loop or the 'statement' part is carried out once before the test is made. This can be useful in certain cases where the programmer knows that a certain course of action has to be carried out at least once. Program number 8 could have been written using this command instead. It is shown below. The main difference is in the relative positions of the component parts of the program, but these do, however, follow the logic of the command. The formal syntax is also shown.

```
        do   statement   while (expression);
```

```
/* program 8a an introduction to do....while */

main()

{
int a;
a = 1;
do
        {
        printf("this is an example of a while condition\n  ");
        a = a + 1;
        }
while(a <= 10);
}
```

The SWITCH-CASE statement.

Frequently in programming a series of logical decisions have to be made. When the if......else command is used these long decision constructions become complex from the programming point of view and complex for the compiler to keep track of. Consider the problems in determining if a particular key press was a vowel, or a consonant, or a numeral, or a punctuation mark. The number of nested if.....else commands needed to sort out that little lot would be quite large. C provides us with a very neat method of coping with such a problem, that also has the advantage of producing a much faster piece of code than would otherwise have been possible. This is the switch-case command. Its formal syntax is shown below.

switch (expression) { (switch-statement) };

This command is one of the most useful for multiple decision tables, since it is relatively easy to code (once you know how) and produces very efficient code. The best possible way to illustrate it is by means of a simple example. This is program 9 and is shown below.

```
/* Program 9 a simple example of switch-case */

#include stdio/csh;

int c;
main()
{
        while((c = getchar()) != EOF)
        {
            printf("you pressed %c\n",c);
            switch (c) {

        case '0':
        case '1':
        case '2':
        case '3':
        case '4':
        case '5':
        case '6':
        case '7':
        case '8':
        case '9':
                printf("its a numeral \n");
                break;
        default:
                printf("its a not a numeral that i know\n");
                break;
                }
        }
}
```

Before we look at the switch-case command itself we will have to examine a very common form of the while.... loop that occurs in program 9 and will occur in many of our programs from now on. This is the while((c = getchar()) ! = EOF) statement. It is an example of an expression which in C can be anything from a simple command through to a complex and convoluted series of multiple commands and statements. If we consider the above expression to be in the form :

while((AAA) != EOF)

we can look at each part in turn. The AAA part contained in brackets will be carried out first. We put it in brackets to force the compiler to carry out this part of the expression before any other, and also to avoid the possibility of confusion. It is very similar to the use of brackets in algebra. In our example the AAA part was c=getchar, which simply assigns the value of the key pressed to c. The != part of the command means 'is not equal to' and is a standard C command. It is identical to <> in BASIC. Or .NE. in FORTRAN. The EOF is another standard C term and in our present example refers to the <BREAK> key on TANDY machines or the <CTRL-C> key on CP/M machines. In other words, the section of code will keep being executed until the <BREAK> or <CTRL-C> keys are pressed. We could express this command in the following way (this is often referred to as pseudocode and is an alternative to using flowcharts).

> while c is not EOF
> do the following statements;

As we saw earlier this single line is very useful since it allows the program to continue and possibly respond to any key, but to terminate if the <BREAK> or <CTRL-C> keys are pressed. We could, of course, have used any other key to terminate the program e.g.

while((c=getchar()) !='q')

to make the program terminate when 'q' was typed. This would, however, be of limited value in our present examples.

Now that the somewhat complex while..... expression has been explained we are free to look at the switch-case command in more detail.

Program 9 starts with the #include stdio/csh; statement which as mentioned earlier simply includes some standard definitions in with the program. As we said before this is simply to stop us having to redefine the characters used to represent a new line, end of file and so on, each time that we write a program. The next statement defines c to be an integer and the rest of the program is taken up with the function main(). The first statement of main() is our while expression, and this executes the remainder of the function while the <BREAK> or <CTRL-C> keys are not pressed. The statements following the while expression are multiple statements and are enclosed in a pair of braces. In other words everything within these braces will be carried out until the terminating key is pressed.

The first statement within these braces is a printf() command and this prints the message onto the screen. The only difference between this and previous versions of the printf() command is that this one uses the %c formatting instruction. This tells the compiler that the variable c is to be printed on screen as a character. Although we have defined it as an integer it will be treated as a character for screen display purposes. (This apparent anomaly will be explained later).

The next statement is the first of the switch-case command. This simply says switch (c) and then an open brace. The way in which it works is by telling the compiler to use the switch-case command using c as the variable. Remember that we said that switch-case was used instead of multiple if....else statements. Thinking of the variable as the item being tested the case ' ': part of the statement corresponds to the various alternatives that are being tested for. In our example everything within the pair of braces following the switch(c) command is going to be tested for. But what are we testing for ?

Our relatively simple program is going to test the key value and tell us if it was a numeral (number key) or not. So we test the variable against all possible digits (0.....9), and print out one message if a match is found or another if no match is found.

The switch-case in our example breaks down into two parts: the first contains all the digits in a standard format (case '0':) the slash marks contain the character tested for. The case and colon are compulsory. Following these is the message that is to be printed if a match is found, this is a printf() command as before. This is followed by a break; statement which will be executed if a match is found. It simply prevents the program from 'falling through' to the next section. The default: command specifies what is to happen if a match does not occur. In this case another message will be printed and another break is forced.

The most important points to note are (1) the various alternatives that are tested for are all contained in a pair of braces, after the initial switch() statement, (2) Each condition tested for must be explicitly stated in the form of a case xxx: statement, where xxx represents the condition tested for, (3) A break; statement must follow each outcome to prevent the program 'falling through', (4) A default statement should be present to allow for any 'unforeseen' outcomes to the test.

Program 9 'CP/M' is the listing for running on the 16bit (CP/M) compiler. We have not used the standard input/output file to define EOF because this sets EOF equal to -1. This value is fine for use with disk files but does not help with <CTRL-C>, which returns a value of 3. To enable us to use this key to terminate the program we have defined EOF to be equal to 3. In this way the main loop of the program will terminate whenever the <CTRL-C> key is pressed. The full use of the #define command will be explained in detail further on.

```
/* Program 9 CP/M a simple example of switch-case */

#define EOF 3
```

```
int c;
main()
{
        while((c = getchar()) != EOF)
          {
            printf("you pressed %c\n",c);
            switch (c) {
            case '0':
            case '1':
            case '2':
            case '3':
            case '4':
            case '5':
            case '6':
            case '7':
            case '8':
            case '9':
                printf("its a numeral \n");
                break;
            default:
                printf("its a not a numeral that i know \n");
                break;
                        }
          }
}
```

Apart from the one simple change the two programs are identical. This is one of the strong points about the C language. It is very machine and processor independent.

We will look at another simple example of the switch-case command before we look at a more sophisticated program. Let us consider a possible five way test. If our variable (we will use an integer called c) is one of five values a particular function will be called up. If it is some other value then a warning message will be printed out. Program 9b shows this.

```
/* program 9b a different version of switch case */

        switch (c) {
        case 560:
            first();
            break;
        case 123:
            second();
            break;
        case 637:
            third():
            break;
        case 245:
            fourth();
```

```
        break;
    case 109:
        fifth();
        break;
    default:
        printf("WARNING THIS VALUE IS NOT CORRECT \n");
        break;
        }
```

In the program 9b the functions are assumed to have been defined in another part of the program, together with any other relevant definitions etc. Also the case values were not contained in ' ' marks. This is because in program 9 we were interested in testing for the characters represented by the integer value of c. In program 9b we are testing for a particular integer value, not the character corresponding to that value.

The vertical layout of the case xxx: alternatives is not compulsory, we could write them as:

case '0': case '1': case '2':........ etc.

But this rapidly leads to programs which are difficult to understand and the vertical layout is to be preferred.

Program 10 is a more sophisticated example of switch-case and is used to illustrate a relatively involved problem for the if....else command.

The problem is to test for a key-press and print out a message telling the user if the key was a vowel, semi-vowel, numeral, consonant, punctuation mark, or some other unidentified symbol. The program is given below, and apart from a few comments should be self explanatory.

```
/* Program 10 a real switch-case example */

#include stdio/csh;

int key;
main()
{
        while((key = getchar()) != EOF)
          {
            clear();
            printf("you pressed %c \n",key);
            switch (key) {
            case 'a':
            case 'e':
            case 'i':
            case 'o':
            case 'u':
```

```
                printf("it's a vowel ok \n");
                break;
        case 'w':
        case 'y':
                printf("it's a semi-vowel.\n");
                break;
        case ',':
        case '.':
        case ';':
        case ':':
        case '!':
        case '?':
        case '"':
        case '(':
        case ')':
        case '/':
                printf("it's a punctuation mark\n");
                break;
        case '0':
        case '1':
        case '2':
        case '3':
        case '4':
        case '5':
        case '6':
        case '7':
        case '8':
        case '9':
                printf("it's a numeral \n");
                break
        default:
            if(key >= 'a' && key <= 'z' ) printf("its a consonant \n");
            else
               printf("it's a rather strange character\n");
            break;
                        }
        }
}

clear()
{
  fill( 15360, 1023,32 );
  cursor(0,0);
}
```

The program is essentially the same as our two previous examples with one or two additions. The clear screen function will be used throughout the book. It uses the fill() command which will be explained in detail later on. What it does in this case is to take a block of memory (one that corresponds to the screen) and fill it with ASCII character 32's. These represent blanks and the effect of this is to clear the screen. The first number inside the brackets corresponds to the start of the memory block, the second number represents the number of memory locations to be filled and the final number corresponds to the character that will be placed in the memory locations. In our example the first number is the memory location of the top left hand corner of the screen, which is 1023 characters in size. The second command cursor(0,0) resets the cursor to the top left hand corner of the screen.

There are five sections to the program, with each one corresponding to the occurrence of (1) vowels, (2) semi-vowels, (3) punctuation marks, (4) numerals and (5) others.

The final section dealing with 'others' in fact covers two possibilities. The first is that the key pressed was a consonant, ie, is between the letters 'a' and 'z'. The second is that some unknown key was pressed. This decision is made by means of an if....else command, since this simple two way decision is easier to implement using if....else than by writing out all the consonants in a switch-case construction. There is a new symbol in the if statement, this is the logical and symbol '&&'. The command.

if(key >= 'a' && key <= 'z')printf("xxx");

means that if variable key is greater than or equal to 'a' AND is less than or equal to 'z' then the message printf("xxx") will be printed. In other words, it must be a consonant, because it is not a vowel and it is not a semi-vowel.

The exact positioning of the pairs of braces is important. The outermost pair correspond to the function main(). They are the delimiters for this function. The second pair correspond to the statements of the while....command and delimit these. The innermost pair correspond to the switch-case command and delimit all the statements belonging to this.

```
/* Program 10 CP/M a real switch-case example */

#define EOF 3

int key;
main()
{
     while((key = ci()) != EOF)
       {
         clear();
         printf("you pressed %c\n",key);
         switch (key) {
         case 'a':
         case 'e':
         case 'i':
         case 'o':
         case 'u':
```

19

```
                       printf("it's a vowel ok\n");
                       break;
            case 'w':
            case 'y':
                       printf("it's a semi-vowel\n");
                       break;
            case ',':
            case '.':
            case ';':
            case ':':
            case '!':
            case '?':
            case '"':
            case '(':
            case ')':
            case '/':
                       printf("it's a punctuation mark \n");
                       break;
            case '0':
            case '1':
            case '2':
            case '3':
            case '4':
            case '5':
            case '6':
            case '7':
            case '8':
            case '9':
                       printf("it's a numeral\n");
                       break;
            default:
                  if(key >= 'a' && key <= 'z' ) printf("it's a consonant\n");
                  else
                     printf("it's a rather strange character \n");
                  break;
                                 }
              }
}

clear()
{
     scr_clr();
     scr_rowcol(0,0);
}
```

There are three differences between the LC and DeSmet versions of this program. The first is that the EOF character has been defined as being a 3, the second is that the key = getchar() statement has been replaced by the key = ci() one. The main reason for this is that the getchar() statement echoes the character onto the screen, the ci() command does not. Apart from this they are exactly the same. We will see later on that the LC compiler stops the screen echo in a different way. The final difference is that the clear screen function clear() uses two different commands on the 16 bit compiler. The first of these clears the screen and the second takes the cursor to the top left hand corner of the screen.

We have now covered the most complex, but the most powerful of the control statements in C. We have one more to look at and this is the for... command.

The FOR statement.

This statement is useful but rather strange in that its job can easily be done with a while ..... command. The formal syntax is shown below:-

for(expr-1 ; expr-2 ; expr-3) statement;

It is a control loop and expr-1 ..... expr-3 correspond to acceptable C expressions. The statement part can be a simple one command statement or a series of multiple statements enclosed in braces. The loop works by evaluating expr-1 (setting the initial parameters), testing against expr-2 (testing the end condition at the start of each execution), then carrying out whatever is contained in the statement part, and executing expr-3 at the end of the statement (adjusting whatever is contained in this expression, normally some form of counter). The second expression is then tested (expr-2) and if true the loop is re-executed and the process continues until expr-2 is tested and found false.

The way in which this loop could be written in a while.... command is shown below:

```
expr-1;
while (expr-2)
{
        statement;
        expr-3;
}
```

It is up to the individual programmer which particular form of this control loop is used. In a number of applications there seems to be little or no difference to the speed of execution or to the legibility of the programs using either method.

One relatively simple example will demonstrate the statement's use. This is shown in program 11, which prints out the letters of the alphabet onto the screen.

```
/*Program 11 an alphabetic listing */

int letter;
main()
{
        clear();
        for(letter = 'a' ; letter <= 'z' ; letter = letter + 1)
```

21

```
                        putchar(letter);
}

clear()
{
    fill( 15360,1023,32 );
    cursor(0,0);
}
```

This program should be self explanatory, the only new point is the use of putchar() to output the variable letter onto the screen. It is essentially the output version of getchar() and is used in a similar way.

The CP/M version of program 11 is shown below. The only difference between the two is in the screen handling functions. These are identical to the previous program's.

```
/*Program  11 CP/M an alphabetic listing */

int letter;
main()
{
        clear();
        for(letter = 'a' ; letter <= 'z' ; letter = letter + 1)
                            putchar(letter);
}

clear()
{
    scr_clr();;
    scr_rowcol(0,0);
}
```

Before we finish this chapter we must mention three methods of terminating loops and functions. One of these we have already seen. These three methods are the BREAK, CONTINUE and RETURN statements.

The break statement has already been seen in the switch-case programs, and as stated before is used to exit any part of the statement to prevent the program 'falling through'. In addition the break statement can be used to exit any while, do or for loop.

The continue statement is used to jump over or skip the remaining statements in a compound loop. It will be used in later programs where it will be explained further.

The return statement can be in one of two forms. These are shown below:

return;
return expression;

It is used to end a currently executing function. Normally the function would end at the final line, as if a simple return were present. If, under some set of conditions we wanted the function to terminate before the end then this could be achieved by the use of a return statement.

The return expression; statement is used whenever we want to terminate a function and to pass back to the main program whatever is the value of expression. For example, if we wanted to declare a function to square a number we could call the function "square(numb)", where numb was some integer, then the function could be defined as:

$$\text{square(numb)}$$
$$\{ \text{ return numb * numb ; } \}$$

Here every time the function is called it returns the value of numb * numb. (the * symbol means multiply, exactly the same as in BASIC). This is a particularly useful feature if the variables used throughout the program are local ones. (The meaning of local variables will be explained later on).

SUMMARY OF CHAPTER 2.

(1)   All the control loops in C were introduced. These are the if.....else, while....., do....while, switch-case, for..., statements.

(2)   The three methods of exiting from loops and functions were introduced. These are the break; , continue; , and return; statements.

(3)   In addition, various aspects of the C language were introduced wherever necessary. These are summarised below:

    (A)   integer definition using the int c; command, where c is an integer variable.

    (B)   The use of the #include stdio/csh; command to load in standard functions for use throughout the program.

    (C)   Compound expressions making use of the definition of EOF to mean either the <BREAK> or <CTRL-C> keys.
        These definitions are contained in the stdio/csh functions.

    (D)   Use of the && operator for logical AND tests.

    (E)   Use of the != operator meaning NOT EQUAL TO.

    (F)   Use of the <= operator meaning less than or equal to.

    (G)   Use of the >= operator meaning greater than or equal to.

    (H)   Use of the * operator to mean multiply.

    (I)   The putchar() statement to output a character to the standard output device (defined in stdio/csh as the screen).

Chapter 3

Data Types and Operators.

In the previous chapters we have looked at the various ways in which simple C programs can be written. We will now go on to look at the different data types that are available to C programmers and also the various operators that can be used with them. An operator is simply a symbol that represents an operation on one or more data items. Some examples that we have already used are the '*' operator meaning multiply and the operators '>=' and '<=' meaning greater than or equal to, and less than or equal to, respectively.

DATA TYPES: CONSTANTS.

With most of this chapter there will be slight differences from one compiler to another. The exact representation of certain data constants or data types may vary, so too will various extensions and limitations. The majority of this chapter deals with the LC compiler, with the corresponding conventions for the DeSmet compiler being dealt with in the appendix. You are warned to consult your compiler manual for precise details of how your compiler handles some of these data constants and conventions.

As with most computer languages C expects numbers and characters to be entered in certain ways and according to certain rules. This enables the compiler to understand them and to act accordingly. Any data item that is fixed in value throughout a program is called a constant.

Numerical constants are entered exactly as we would expect, if we are dealing with decimal numbers. Two other number bases are supported by LC, these are octal and hexadecimal. The octal and hexadecimal notation are relatively standard in C compilers.

To indicate to the compiler that the number in question is in another base it is represented with a leading zero. A leading zero followed by a string of digits represents an octal number, if the leading zero is followed by either a 'X' or an 'x' then the number is hexadecimal. The following table should make this clear.

DECIMAL	OCTAL	HEXADECIMAL
100	0144	0x64
23	027	0x17
349	0535	0x15D
7	07	0x7
42	052	0x2A

Character constants are represented by enclosing the character in single quote marks. The data stored in the computer's memory is the integer representing the character. Most microcomputers use the ASCII character code and so the letter 'A' would be stored as 65 (decimal) in the computer's memory.

This is why, in our switch-case programs, we were able to accept a keyboard input as an integer quantity and test this against a list of character constants. What the compiler was doing was to convert the characters into their corresponding integer representations and then test the input value.

A brief word of warning. The compiler does not test for the number of characters between the quotes. It is possible to assign too many characters to a particular variable and in this case only the last one or two will be used. It is up to the programmer to allow for this in the programs. There is also no test for numeric values. As with most computer systems there is a limit to the upper value that a particular integer variable may store. If an overload takes place then the compiler simply stores the Least Significant Bits (LSB) of the number. This is, in effect, the remainder after the number has been divided by 256. The compiler gives no warning or error status of this and once again it is left to the individual programmer to check the source code for any possible errors.

If a sequence of character values has to be stored in a data constant then the double quotes (" ") must be used to enclose the characters or data string. The variable being used to store the string must be of a suitable size to allow the full length of the string plus one extra character to indicate the end of the data item. The following table should make this clear.

DATA STRING	TOTAL NUMBER OF CHARACTERS
"This is an example"	19
"Another test"	13
"C is a very interesting language."	34

What the compiler stores is not a complete list of the characters in a variable but simply the address of the first character in the list. By the use of pointers (a very useful feature of C) we are able to manipulate both the string and the memory locations of the string.

In some of our later programs we used a statement line that loaded a number of standard library routines into our programs. This statement was #include stdio/csh; and one of the functions that it performs is to define the standard control characters that are required by any computer to control input and output to printers,screen,keyboard etc. These are usually referred to as ESCAPE CHARACTERS and will be defined for each machine in turn. By having the definitions in a standard library (written by the compiler writers for each computer) the C language is made much more transportable. The table below gives the conventions used in LC. Again the character codes used by most microcomputers and many mainframes is the ASCII code.

ESCAPE SEQUENCE	CONTROL CODE	ASCII CODE (LC)
\n, \N	Newline Character	x'0D' CR
\t, \t	Horizontal Tab	x'09' HT
\b, \B	Backspace	x'08' BS
\r, \R	Carriage Return	x'0D' CR
\f, \F	Form Feed	x'0C' FF
\\,	Backslash	x'5C' backslash
\',	Single quote	x'2C' apostrophe
\0,	Null	x'00' null byte
\",	Double quote	x'22' double quote

The above codes can be represented as either normal control characters ie.\t,.\n,.\f, or as octal or hexadecimal codes. The use of octal codes is standard on C compilers, but hexadecimal codes for escape characters is quite unusual. In all of our examples we will only use the standard format of control characters.

VARIABLE DATA.

Having looked at the way in which C handles constant data types, we are in a position to look at variable data. As with all other computer languages C uses names to represent variables, functions and labels. These names are called identifiers and they can vary in length from one character to almost any length. In practice their length will be a trade-off between what is of most use to the programmer and what is practical to keep typing in. Most compilers have a limit to the number of characters that are unique. In LC this is eight so the following data names would all be the same to the compiler.

```
testing1 2345678
testing1 forachange
testing1 again
testing1 23howaboutthat
```

The range of characters that may be used in identifiers is dependent on the compiler being used. Most use the capital letters A to Z and the lower case letters a to z, with the digits 0 to 9. In addition the underline character '_' may be used within an identifier (This means that it cannot be used as the first character of the identifier). The rules governing the acceptable identifier names will vary from compiler to compiler, but a selection of generally acceptable identifiers is given below:

```
            a
            c
            p
            t
        one
        average
        final
        squares
        data_list
        chars_test
        line45chk
         a3
         e43
```

Any data that is going to be used in a program must be declared before use. This is done by declaring a particular identifier to be of a certain data type. The data types that C uses are listed below:

```
    int
    float
    char
    short
    long
    double
```

The data type int means that the variables listed will be integers, float means that they will be floating point or real numbers. The size or precision with which these numbers are handled is dependent on the machine in use. The appropriate manual should be consulted to determine the limitations. Char specifies a character data type. Long, Short and double refer to long integers, short integers and double precision floating point numbers. These are all somewhat confusing since the way in which each compiler handles them can be different. There is no guarantee that a short integer will be any different from a long one or the other way round. The way in which a double precision variable is handled will vary from machine to machine and it is generally twice as long as a float variable.

LC and many microcomputer C implementations store a character variable in eight bits and a numeric variable in sixteen bits. The long and short variable types are also stored in sixteen bits and so are the same as ordinary integers. It is possible to declare an integer as being unsigned. This means that the variable can only be used to handle positive numbers, but it increases the permissible range of the variable. (on a computer using sixteen bit integers) an unsigned integer can range from 0 to 65,535 (decimal) and a signed integer can range from -32,768 to 32,767 (decimal).

Arrays and pointers are allowed for all the data types. We will look at pointers in more detail later on. An array is simply a collection of data variables, with the same name, but having subscripts or indexes to identify them. Arrays have to contain the same type of data. It is possible to have arrays of characters or integers or long integers, but not a mixture of the different types.

In C as with many other languages the array subscripts begin at element number '0'. A five element array called fred[5] would have the following elements:- fred[0], fred[1], fred[2], fred[3], fred[4].

The following table gives some acceptable data declarations.

DATA DECLARATION	VARIABLE NAME	DATA TYPE
char a;	a	character
char z;	z	character
int a,b,c;	a and b and c	all integers
short b;	b	short integer
unsigned f;	f	unsigned integer
char name[20]	name	character array of up to 20 characters
int pay[10]	pay	integer array of up to 10 digits

POINTERS.

It is possible to declare a pointer to a particular data item. But what exactly is a pointer ? Quite simply a pointer is a variable that contains the address of another data item, in other words it literally points to that data item. This is particularly useful when dealing with character arrays, since C has no direct commands for dealing with strings of characters. While this may seem a major disadvantage when compared to a language like BASIC it does mean that the programmer has more direct control over the data variables themselves.

In the following sequence we will define a character array and assign a pointer to the first element of the array.

28

```
          char test[100];
          char *cp;
          cp = test[0]  /* remember element 0 is the first element in an array
*/;
```

Here test is our character array and cp is a pointer to a character. By using *var, var becomes a pointer to a particular data item. Some examples of pointers are given below.

POINTER DECLARATION	POINTERS IDENTIFIER	ITEM POINTED TO
char *cp	cp	character
int *d	d	integer
char *pointer	pointer	character
int *number	number	integer

Using the definitions above we could use the pointers to give us either the address of the data item or the data item itself. For instance, with the pointer *cp using *cp = 'a' will store the character a in the address pointed to by cp, using cp = 18950 the address pointed to by cp is 18950 (decimal).

We will look at pointers in more detail throughout the book but for the time being a simple program will help us to understand what the pointers are all about.

The program sequence is listed below. It is a function called fill() and is called from the main program by fill(a) where a is the address of a data buffer area (more about that later). For now, consider the buffer area to be a character array of suitable size to hold all the data being typed. The value of a would be the first element of the array.

```
     fill(a)
     char*a;
     {
         while (( c = getchar()) != eol && != EOF)
             {
                 *a = c  /* line comment 1 */;
                 a = a + 1  /* line comment 2 */;
             }
             *cp = NULL  /* line comment 3 */;
             return c;
     }
```

In our example variable a contains the current address of a data array and would be passed to fill() by a standard function call. Our multiple expression line is back again with one addition. The != eol && != EOF mean that variable c will be tested against the <ENTER> (RETURN) key and against the <BREAK> <CTRL-C> key. If either has been pressed then the while...... loop is terminated. The expression could be interpreted as follows: while c is not equal to the end of line (eol) and is not equal to the end of file (EOF) do the statements.

We have defined variable a as being a pointer to a character by the char *a definition. If one of the two end conditions have not been met then the loop statements are carried out. Comment line 1 assigns the value of variable c to the memory address pointed to by *a. Comment line 2 then increases the value of the pointer a (i.e. increases the address by 1) and the loop continues. In this way the array or buffer area is gradually filled with the characters typed in until one of the two exit conditions is met.

When the exit conditions are met the next part of the array is set to a NULL value by the *a = NULL. This simply places an end of array marker in place. The function returns with the current value of variable c.

OPERATORS.

C makes use of a number of operators, far more than are normally available in a computer language. Some of them will not be used very often in this book since they deal with the manipulation of data in binary form (the bitwise operators). For a full explanation of the way in which these work the reader should consult either the compiler manual or one of the more advanced books on C. A list of all operators is included in the appendices for the sake of completeness.

UNARY OPERATORS.

C has two types of operators. The first type that we will deal with are the unary operators. These act on one object only, as distinct from the binary operators which act on two objects at the same time.

The following are the only unary operators that will be used in the book:

OPERATOR	OBJECT	DESCRIPTION
*	expression	indirection, means "object at..."
&	lvalue	pointer, means "address of..."
!	expression	logical complement, means "not expression"
++	lvalue	increment and save in lvalue
--	lvalue	decrement and save in lvalue

In the above table "expression" means any valid C expression, and lvalue means an expression which when evaluated gives the address of a data item or of a pointer. Some of the above operators have been seen before and will not be discussed further.

The & operator.

This is similar in function to the * operator and delivers the address of a data element. If an array has been declared of size 100 and name "data" then the following would be valid uses of the & operator:

&data[9]   to give the address of the 10th element.
&data[90] to give the address of the 91st element.

similarly the address of a data element defined as int a; could be found by using &a;.

The ++ operator.

In our previous examples the expression a = a + 1 was used to indicate that variable a was to be incremented by 1. The ++ operator does the same thing. So instead of a = a + 1 we would write ++a. This is clearly time saving in program writing although it is very confusing to anyone new to C.

The -- operator.

This functions in a similar way to the ++ operator but it decrements the lvalue. So instead of a = a - 1 we would write -- a.

Prefix and Postfix.

Both the -- and ++ operators can be placed before or after the lvalue. Their position determines the exact way in which they function. When placed before they function as above. When placed after the lvalue the value of the lvalue is incremented after it is used. The subtle difference between the two can be seen in the following table:

31

PREFIX EXPRESSION	POSTFIX EXPRESSION	STARTING A	VALUE B	FINAL A	VALUE B
a = ++b	------	2	4	5	5
------	a = b++	2	4	4	5
a = --b	------	2	4	3	3
------	a = b--	2	4	4	3

In almost all of our examples and programs only prefix use of the ++ and -- operators will be made.

BINARY OPERATORS.

Binary operators, as stated before, act on two expressions. The result that is generated depends on the types of the two expressions. There are various conventions governing the precedence of these operators and their effect on pointers. Where required, we will explain these peculiarities as we come to them in our programs. Again we will only cover a limited range of operators, the reader should consult the manuals or other texts for a detailed explanation of those we have missed out.

TABLE OF BINARY OPERATORS

OPERATOR	ACTION
*	multiplication
/	division
%	modulus (remainder)
+	addition
−	subtraction
<	less than
>	greater than
<=	less than or equal to
>=	greater than or equal to
==	equal to
!=	not equal to
&&	logical and
||	logical or
?:	equivalent to if..then..else

In all of the above cases (with the exception of the last) the general format is <exp1> OP <exp2> where <exp1> means expression number 1, OP is the relevant operator and <exp2> is expression number 2. Some of the above are obvious while others have been dealt with before. We will now look at the remainder.

The % operator.

The / operator only uses integer division (i.e. no remainder is produced). To obtain a remainder, or to check if one is produced, the % operator is used. So if variables a and b represent two integer values the statement z = a % b will place the remainder of the division into variable z.

The || operator.

This is the second binary logical operator and is used in the same way as the OR command in BASIC or the .OR. command in FORTRAN. It would be used in any logical decision requiring an "or" condition, for example, with variable c representing an integer the following test could be carried out.

```
if( c == 'a' || c == 'e' || c == 'i' || c == 'o' || c == 'u')
  {
     printf('it's a vowel\n');
  }
```

In this way variable c is tested for each of the vowel characters in turn. If any of the tests is true then the message is printed out.

The ?: operator.

This is a rather odd operator in that it can be used to represent the if...then...else construct. Its use is illustrated below.

```
p = a ? b : c ;
```

Here the letters represent the relevant data types. In the present example p is set equal to the value of b if the value of a is non zero. If a is zero then p is set equal to the value of c.

An IMPORTANT note.

C distinguishes between the equality operator == and the assignation operator =. Some languages (BASIC) do not. The use of the wrong operator can cause some interesting results.

Summary of Chapter 3.

(1)   The use of data constants to represent various control codes.

(2)   The various types of identifiers allowed by C.

(3)   Data variables and data types used by C.

(4)   Pointers and their uses.

(5)   Unary operators.

(6)   Binary operators.

Chapter 4

Program Examples.

Now that we have seen most of the essential commands in C we are in a position to write and examine some real programs. These are rather simple but they will enable us to study some of the more subtle problems and their possible solutions. Our first program example is Program 12. This is a first attempt to produce a multiplication table.

What we are trying to do is to accept any integer (within a certain range) from the keyboard and then produce the corresponding multiplication table from it. We will only produce the first twelve iterations (repeated calculations) of the table as this is all that is reasonably needed. The principle, once developed, could of course be extended to further ranges of tables and any number of iterations.

```
/* Program 12 Multiplication Tables */

#include stdio/csh;
#define NL printf("\n")
#define PARA printf("\n\n\n")
int c,i,t,d;
main()
c = 1;
while ( c != EOF )
   {
    printf("Please enter the table you require ");
    c =getchar();
    NL;
    i = 1;
    while ( i <= 12 )
      {
       t = i*c;
       printf(" %c X %d = %d\n",c,i,t);
       ++i;
      }
    PARA;
   }
}
```

Our first attempt is a fairly short program and it consists mainly of C terms that we have encountered before. The first program line is the #include stdio/csh; line which causes the standard definitions to be loaded with the program. The following two lines are new. The #define NL printf("\n") and #define PARA printf("\n\n\n") statements mean that any occurrence of NL in a program line will be interpreted as a /n command. Similarly any occurrence of PARA will be interpreted as \n \n \n.

This illustrates the use of the #define command to predefine any commonly used statements and make their entry in the program much easier. The #define statements can be of any length up to the limits of the system. In some compilers it is possible to nest definitions to produce complex definitions. We will not use these in any of our programs.

The next section of the program declares the variables c,i,t, and d to be integers. Function main() starts with the command c = 1;. This sets the integer c to be equal to 1 as a precaution against it assuming a value equal to EOF at runtime.

The while loop is executed as long as the value of variable c is not EOF. Unlike previous examples the c = getchar; part of this complex expression is not within the while command. The main reason for this is that it allows the body of the while statement to be executed once before waiting for the key press. As an alternative we could have used the do.....while command.

The printf() statement causes the message to be printed onto the screen and the c = getchar accepts the response and assigns the value to variable c. NL forces a new line and i = 1; assigns the value 1 to variable i.

The next section of the program is the loop that produces twelve iterations of the multiplication table. By using the command while (i <= 12) the body of the loop is executed until variable i becomes greater than 12. The statement t = i * c; calculates the product of variables i and c and assigns the product to variable t.

Following the calculation part of the loop the printf() command displays the sum and the result onto the screen. We have already seen some of the actions that the printf() command can produce but we will examine this line in detail.

The command line printf("%cX%d = %d\n",c,i,t); means that the variable c will be printed as a character (%c), this will be followed by a space and the the symbol X (representing the multiplication sign). Variable i is then printed after a space and in decimal notation. This is followed by a space, an equals sign and then another space. The final variable (t) is then printed as a decimal.

Following the printf() line the variable i is incremented using prefix notation of the ++ operator. This process is continued until variable i is over 12. The second loop is ended and the predefined command PARA prints three line feeds on the screen. If c was equal to EOF the program will terminate, if not the first message is printed onto the screen and the c = getchar() command waits for the key-press. This whole process is continued until the <BREAK> or <CTRL-C> key is pressed.

```
/* Program 12 CP/M Multiplication Tables */
#define NL printf(" \n")
#define PARA printf("\n \n \n")
#define EOF 3
int c,i,t,d;
main()
c = 1;
while ( c != EOF )
    {
    printf("Please enter the table you require");
    c = getchar();
    NL;
    i = 1;
    while ( i <= 12 )
      {
        t = i*c;
        printf(" %c X %d = %d\n",c,i,t);
        ++i;
      }
    PARA;
    }
}
```

The CP/M version of program 12 is very similar except for the exclusion of the #include statement and the definition of the EOF label. The main body of the program functions in exactly the same way as before.

If the program is run three main points come to light.

(1)   The program does NOT work.
(2)   If <BREAK> or <CTRL-C> is pressed the program continues for one
        sequence.
(3)   Only one digit integers can be entered at any time.

We will deal with the first two of these points.

(1) The fact that the program does not work will not be of great surprise to those readers who remembered that the c = getchar() command returns an integer value that corresponds to the key pressed. As such any arithmetic operation carried out on this value will not directly relate to the same operation carried out on the digit represented by the key. The following is an example of the type of screen display produced by the program.

```
2   X   1   =   50
2   X   2   =   100
2   X   3   =   150
```

```
5   X   1   =   53
5   X   2   =   106
5   X   3   =   159
```

We attempt to solve this in the second program in this chapter, by subtracting the integer value corresponding to '0' from the integer value of the key pressed. This has the effect of reducing any digit key value down to the actual integer represented by the key. It works because the digit and their integer representations are in an ascending sequence starting with the digit '0'. The statement that does this is I = c - '0'; (remember that we use '0' rather than just 0 to subtract the integer value of the '0' digit).

The next problem that we have to face is that in the LC compiler, as with a number of the eight bit compilers, the range of the arithmetic operations that the simple binary operators (*, /, +, -) can work on is limited, so any methods that we introduce here will be of little use if we restrict ourselves to these operators.

Fortunately LC provides us with a range of powerful arithmetic functions that act on both single precision and double precision numbers. In most of our work we will use single precision only. The range of values that can be supported by the double and single precision commands will vary from one compiler to another. Once again consult your manual for the precise details. We will look at each of the commands in turn as we come to them.

The CP/M compiler, being a sixteen bit implementation of C does not have these restrictions on floating point numbers. Due to this the programs using floating point statements will be somewhat simpler in the CP/M versions. The majority of 'full' implementations of C will have floating point arithmetic capability as standard.

(2) The second problem, that the program continues through one complete loop before exiting is easily solved by the use of the if(c == EOF) exit(0); command. This causes the program to exit if the EOF condition is met. The exit(0) statement (on the LC compiler) means that no error code will be generated on the return to the operating system.

We could have used the do....while command instead but the problem is just as easily solved by the above method.

The program listing is shown in program 13.

```
/* program 13 multiplication tables improved vII */

#include stdio/csh;
int c,i,t,d,l;
char N1[4];
char N2[4];
char ANS[8];
```

```
#define NL printf("\n")
#define PARA printf("\n\n\n")
#option FPLIB
main()
{
    c = 1;
    while (c != EOF)
    {
        printf("Please enter the table you require ");
        c = getchar();
        if( c == EOF ) exit(0);
        NL;
        i = 1;
        l = c - '0';
        while ( i <= 12 )
          {
            itof( l, N2 );
            itof( i, N1 );
            fmul( N2, N1 );
            ftoa( N2, ANS );
            printf(" %c X %.4d = %.8s\n",c,i,ANS);
            ++i;
          }
        PARA;
    }
}
```

Essentially programs 12 and 13 are very similar. There are some differences apart from the minor modifications explained above. (1) Three character arrays are declared, N1 and N2 both of four bytes length and ANS of eight bytes length. These are required to store the results of the data conversion functions.

(2) Another #option is included. This is the #option FPLIB and includes the floating point library into the program. Without this library we would be unable to use the extra functions and would be limited to those functions that we have written ourselves.

We have now covered all of the modifications to program 12 except the use of the floating point functions.

The three functions that we use are as follows:- itof, fmul, ftoa.

itof(l, N2);	Is the integer to single precision conversion function. It takes integer l and places a single precision value in array N2.
itof(i, N1);	Does the same as above to i and N1.
fmul(N2, N1);	Is the single precision multiplication function and multiplies the single precision numbers N2 and N1 the result of this operation is then placed in N2.

ftoa(N2, ANS);   Converts the single precision number N2 into an
                                    ASCII string. This is necessary to allow us to be able
                                    to print out the answer onto the screen.

The printf() is similar to our previous examples except that the final command
'%.8s\n' prints a string onto the screen and the .8 command tells the compiler the
maximum number of string bytes to print.

Some sample screen output for program 13 is given below.

        2   X   1   =   2
        3   X   4   =   12
        3   X   3   =   9

        d   X   1   =   52
        d   X   2   =   104
        s   X   3   =   201

The first sample output shows that the program is working for single key digit
input. But what if we enter some alphabetic key? In this case the program still
functions and subtracts '0' from the integer value and then produces the
multiplication table.

```
/* program 13 CP/M multiplication tables improved vll */

int c,i,t,d,l;
int ANS;
#define NL printf("\n")
#define PARA printf("\n\n\n")
#define EOF 3
main()
{
   c = 1;
   while ( c != EOF )
   {
     printf("Please enter the table you require ");
     c = getchar();
     if( c == EOF ) exit(0);
     NL;
     i = 1;
     l = c - '0';
     while ( i <= 12 )
       {
         ANS = l * i;
         printf(" %c X %.4d = %.8s \n",c,i,ANS);
         ++i;
       }
```

```
    PARA;
  }
}
```

The major modifications to program 13 occur in the second loop. In program 13 this loop contained a series of floating point and data conversion functions. Since the CP/M compiler does not require these (it can handle floating point calculations as standard) we are able to use the standard arithmetic operators. In this particular example one statement (ANS = I * i) replaces the four corresponding ones in program 13. This should illustrate how much easier it is to write arithmetic programs with a compiler that deals with floating point operations as standard.

We have to make some further modifications to our 'simple' multiplication program to overcome the main limitation, that only single digits can be entered. The program listing for this final multiplication program is shown in program 14.

```
/* program 14 a final multiplication table */

#include stdio/csh;
#option FPLIB
#option KBECHO OFF
#option INLIB
int c,i,t;
char a[4];
char b[4];
char d[4];
char e[4];
char ans[8];
char no2[8];
main()
{
    c = 1;
    while( c != EOF)
    {
    clear();
    printf("please enter the table you require ");
    fgets( &a[0],4,stdin);
    clear();
    printf("YOUR TABLE IS AS FOLLOWS :-\n");
    for(i=1;i<=12;++i)
    {
      atof( &a[0],d );
      itof( i, e );
      ftoa( d, no2);
      fmul( d, e);
      ftoa( d,ans);
      printf("%-3.3d  X  %-8.8s  =  %s \n",i,no2,ans);
    }
```

```
        printf("------------------------------------\n");
        printf("type <any key> to continue <BRK> to end");
        c = getchar();
        printf("\n");
        }
}
clear()
{
    fill(15360, 1023, 32);
    cursor(0, 0);
}
```

Program 14 is our final multiplication table program. It contains a number of modifications over the original one. The main one is in the way in which the table number is entered into the program. To overcome the problems mentioned earlier the fgets() function is used. This will be explained as we come to it in the program details.

As in program 13 various character arrays have been declared, these are all designed to hold the relevant single precision numbers, products of the multiplication or the data string that contains the original number.

Three options are declared, #option FPLIB; is the same as before, #option KBECHO OFF; turns the keyboard echo off. This means that the key pressed will not be printed onto the screen. It simply serves to tidy up the screen displays, #option INLIB includes some additional functions (cursor control) that will be required in this and successive programs.

The program is divided into two functions, main() and clear(). Function clear() is included to clear the screen and return the cursor to the top left hand corner of the screen. These commands or their equivalents should be available on most C compilers.

fill(15360, 1023, 32); simply fills the memory location starting at 15360 for 1023 bytes. The specified locations are filled with 32 (ASCII blank codes). The overall effect is to clear (blank out) the screen. 15360 is the starting location of the screen and 1023 is the screen size in bytes. The general syntax for this command is :

        fill(abc,xyz,def);

Where abc is the starting address to be filled, xyz is the number of bytes to be filled and def is the decimal value of the character to be placed in there. The final command of this function is cursor(0,0); which places the cursor at the top left hand corner of the screen. The syntax is:

        cursor(c,r);

With c representing the column position and r the row position of the screen. This clear screen function is the same as we have used before. It will be used many times in our LC programs and will not be further explained.

Function main() begins with variable c being set to 1. The while...... command is the same as before. The body of the while... loop starts with a clear() function call and this clears the screen. The message asking the user to enter the table number is then printed onto the screen and this is followed by the fgets(&a[0],4,stdin); statement. We have mentioned this command in passing and will now look at it in more detail.

The syntax of this command is:

      fgets(adr,num,i/o);

Where adr is the address of the string that will hold the data input, num is the number of bytes to be input and i/o is the input device. (in our example stdin represents the standard input device, the keyboard). In our example the address of the string (character array) is given by &a[0]. This delivers the address of the first element of the array and this is used by fgets() as the pointer to the string. The number 4 in our case allows three bytes (key presses) to be entered, this may seem odd because we have used a four byte array. The reason for this is that the compiler will place an end of array marker in the array and so we only have space for 3 bytes in a four byte array. fgets() allows for this by only using num-1 of the bytes to store data, the final byte will be used to store the end of array marker.

So our command fgets() accepts a three byte input from the keyboard into character array a[4].

The next line calls the function clear() and then prints the table heading "YOUR TABLE IS AS FOLLOWS :-". A for..... loop follows this message and this will execute the compound statement twelve times. The structure of this command is exactly the same as our previous examples and will not be explained in any more detail.

We have used one extra data conversion function. This is atof(); and its purpose is to convert the string (pointed to by &a[0]) into the single precision array d. The other functions are as before, but since they are rather new they will be explained again.

itof(i, e); converts the integer i into a single precision number, held in array e.
ftoa(d, no2); converts the single precision number into its ASCII form and this is held in array no2.
fmul(d, e); multiplies the two single precision numbers d and e and places the result into variable d.
ftoa(d, ans); converts the result of the multiplication into the ASCII form and places this in array ans.

The printf() command then displays the sum and the result onto the screen. There are a number of different formats and options used here so we will give the full range of permissible options that can be used with the printf() statement.

printf(control, arg1, arg2.....);

Where control represents a string of print formatting commands. This consists of a number of sub-fields which can be used independently of each other. They are summarised below.

The general layout for the format specifiers is as follows:-

$$\%\{-\}\{xxx\}\{.yyy\}char$$

where

%	= The mandatory indicator for the specification list.
-	= States that the value will be left justified.
xxx	= Minimum width of the print field image.
.yyy	= Maximum number of string bytes to be printed.
char	= The conversion character used. b = binary, o = octal, d = decimal, x = hexadecimal, s = string, c = character, u = unsigned.

According to these formats the values contained in variables i,no2, and ans are printed onto the screen.
Following this a single underline is printed across the screen and another message is displayed. The user's response is taken by the c = getchar() statement. If this is equal to EOF then the program terminates, if some other key is pressed then the program repeats.

If the program is run it will be seen that the results are accurate, and also we have multi-digit (up to three) entry. Another benefit of using the fgets() and atof() commands as data entry statements is that if incorrect keys are pressed (ie non digit keys) the data conversion characters return a value of zero. This goes a good way to correcting our problem of faulty key entry.

```
/* program 14 CP/M a final multiplication table */

int c,i,t;
float ANS;
#define EOF 3

main()
{
   c = 1;
   while( c != EOF)
   {
   clear();
   printf("please enter the table you require ");
   scanf("%d",&t);
   clear();
   printf("YOUR TABLE IS AS FOLLOWS :-\n");
   for(i=1;i<=12;++i)
{
      ANS = i * t;
```

```
    printf("%-3.3d X %-8.8s =    %8.1f \n",i,t,ans);
  }
  printf("--------------------------------------\n");
  printf("type <any key> to continue <CTRL-C> to end");
  c = ci();
  printf("\n");
  }
}
clear()
{
    scr_clr();
    scr_rowcol(0,0);
}
```

There are a number of differences in this program. The comments about the
efficiency of standard floating point commands still apply. Once again we have
replaced five data manipulation and floating point statements with one simple
arithmetic command. Apart from these changes two new statements have been
introduced. The first of these is the scanf("x", add) statement. This acts in a very
similar way to the printf() function, but for data entry. The data is entered into the
variable pointed to by 'add' according to the format indicated by 'x'. Our example
loads the data into variable t, according to the format "%d" (decimal numbar).

The second new statement is the c = ci() command. This works exactly the same as
the c = getchar() statement except that the data entered into the variable is not
echoed onto the screen. In other words there is no equivalent to the #option
KBECHO OFF command of program 14. By using the ci() function the same
results can be obtained.

The only other difference between the two programs is that variable ANS has been
defined as type float (floating point number). This is because with scanf() we could
enter a decimal number. If we did this then the answer to any multiplication would
also be a decimal number. To be able to hold this we have to declare the variable
ANS as such a floating point number. The slight modification to printf() reflects the
fact that we are outputting a floating point number, not a string.

Our final program in this chapter will cover the use of our new functions and input
techniques to produce a four function calculator program.

/* program 15 a calculator */

```
#include stdio/csh;
#option FPLIB
#option INLIB
#option KBECHO OFF
int c,i,c1,s;
char a[6];
char b[6];
```

```
char d[6];
char e[6];
char f[6];
char ans[13];
char no1[9];
char no2[9];
main()
{
    c = 1;
    while( c != EOF)
    {
    clear();
    printf("please enter your two numbers \n");
    fgets( &a[0],6,stdin);
    fgets( &b[0],6,stdin);
    clear();
    atof( b,e);
    atof( a,d );
    atof( a,f );
    printf("------------------------------------- \n");
    cursor(5,10);
    printf("select one of the following functions \n");
    cursor(0,12);
    printf("<A> to add, <S> to subtract, <M> to multiply, <D> to divide.\n");
    printf("in all cases the normal CALCULATOR rules apply\n");
    c1 = getchar();
    if( c1 == 97)aded();
      else
       if( c1 == 115)subt();
        else
        if( c1 == 109)mult();
          else
          if(c1 == 100)divd();
            else
            {
              cursor(0,14);
              printf("WARNING !!!!!! function not recognised ......\n");
            }
    cursor(0,0);
    printf("                ");
    cursor(10,0);
    printf("type <any key> to continue <BRK> to end");
    c = getchar();
    printf("\n");
    }
}
print(f,s,e,ans)
{
    ftoa(d,ans);
```

```
        ftoa(f,no1);
        ftoa(e,no2);
        printf("YOUR SUM WAS --> %-8.8s %c  %-8.8s = %-8.13s\n",no1,s,no2,ans);
        return;
}
clear()
{
        fill( 15360, 1023, 32);
        cursor(0,0);
        return;
}
mult()
{
        fmul( d,e );
        s = 88;
        print(f,s,e,ans);
        return;
}
divd()
{
        fdiv( d,e );
        s = 47;
        print(f,s,e,ans);
        return;
}
aded()
{
        fadd( d,e );
        s = 43;
        print(f,s,e,ans);
        return;
}
subt()
{
        fsub();
        s = 45;
        print(f,s,e,ans);
        return;
}
```

Much of this program will be familiar. The #option commands have all been used before and all of the functions previously introduced are used. The only differences are that some additional single precision operators have been used.

The program asks for two numbers and then displays a range of options, either <A>ddition, <S>ubtraction, <M>ultiplication or <D>ivision can be carried out on the two numbers. When the operation has been executed the user is prompted to press <BRK> to end the program or any other key to continue.

The program structure consists of seven functions, these are:

(1) main()	Acts as the main program body for key responses and program control.
(2) print()	This carries out the data conversions on all the numbers and then outputs them to the screen.
(3) clear()	Is the clear screen function and is the same as described earlier.
(4) mult()	The multiplication function carries out single precision multiplication on the two numbers.
(5) divd()	The division function carries out single precision division on the two numbers.
(6) aded()	The addition function carries out single precision addition on the two numbers.
(7) subt()	The subtraction function carries out single precision subtraction on the two numbers.

There are two groups of functions that are used in this program. These are:-
(1) Functions that act on the two numbers that are to be operated on, these are contained in the arrays d and e. A function call mult() causes the program to execute function mult and to carry out the operation on the numbers contained in variables d and e. In a similar way aded(), subt(), and divd() operate on the same arrays.
(2) The values to be printed, contained in arrays f, e, ans and integer s. Array f contains the first number entered, array e contains the second number entered and array ans contains the product of the operation. Integer s is assigned a value corresponding to the operation symbol to be printed ie 'X' for multiplication, '+' for addition, '-' for subtraction and '/' for division. This technique uses the fact that the printf() command allows us to output an integer variable as its corresponding ASCII symbol.

All of the single precision arithmetic operations have the following format:

operation(a,b);

Where 'operation' is one of the arithmetic operations and a and b represent the operands. In each case the result of the operation is placed into variable a. Some further examples are given below:

OPERATION	VALUES BEFORE OPERATION		VALUES AFTER OPERATION	
	a	b	a	b
fadd(a,b)	3	4	7	4
fsub(a,b)	5	3	2	3
fdiv(a,b)	8	2	4	2
fmul(a,b)	3	4	12	4

Function main() consists of our usual while.... loop with a series of if....else statements. These are to test for the function required by the user.

At the start of the main loop a clear screen call is made by clear(). This clears the screen, places the cursor at the top left hand corner of the screen and in the following line the message "please enter your two numbers " is printed onto the screen.

Two fgets() statements then accept the two numbers from the user into arrays a and b. The same rules for the array sizes and the number of bytes entered apply as in the previous program. The screen is then cleared and the initial data conversions carried out by the use of three atof() commands.

The reason that array a is converted to two single precision numbers is that one of them will be overwritten by the arithmetic operation selected by the user. It is important that we keep a copy of both the original numbers so that the screen display of the sum is correct.

And now, a short note on the use of global and local variables. In all of our programs we will use global variables. This means that we will declare them outside of any functions that we may use. The benefit that we gain from this approach is that we can then access and use any of these variables anywhere in our program. Some other considerations may make individual programmers prefer to use local variables. If this is the case the reader should refer to the compiler manual or to another text to see the effects that these different declarations can have on a program. The CP/M version of program 15 uses local variables and will illustrate the differences in approach that this entails.

After the data conversion functions have been carried out a line is printed on screen and the cursor repositioned. The cursor(5,10) call positions the cursor on row 10 and column 5. The message is then printed, followed by another cursor reposition and a further message. Once all the messages have been displayed a getchar() statement is used to accept the user's response. This places the integer value into variable c_1.

A nested if...else construction follows and it is this that selects the relevant function by testing the value of c_1. The values tested for correspond to the integer representations of A, D, S, and M for addition, division, subtraction and multiplication with a function call if the test is true. Should some other key be pressed then the warning message "WARNING !!!!!! function not recognised " is output to the screen.

The final part of main() is reached after the relevant function calls have been made or after the warning message has been displayed. This part places the cursor at the top left of the screen, prints a blank line, repositions the cursor and then prints the message "type <any key> to continue <BRK> to end". This is then followed by a c = getchar() command to accept the response. As before if <BRK> is pressed the program ends, any other key causes the program to continue.

A final word on the function calls. The main body of the program calls one of the arithmetic functions which in turn calls the print function. At the end of each function the return command transfers control back to the calling function.

```
/* program 15 CP/M  a calculator */

#define EOF 3
main()
{
    float d,e;
    int c,cl,s;
    c = 1;
    while( c != EOF)
    {
    clear();
    printf("please enter your two numbers\n");
    scanf("%f",&d);
    scanf("%f",&e);
    clear();
    printf("-------------------------------------\n");
    cursor(10,5);
    printf("select one of the following functions\n");
    cursor(12,0);
    printf("<A> to add, <S> to subtract, <M> to multiply, <D> to divide.\n");
    printf("in all cases the normal CALCULATOR rules apply \n");
    c1 = ci();
    if( c1 == 97)aded(d,e);
      else
       if( c1 == 115)subt(d,e);
        else
         if( c1 == 109)mult(d,e);
           else
            if(c1 == 100)divd(d,e);
             else
              {
                scr_rowcol(14,0);
                printf("WARNING !!!!!! function not recognised ......\n");
```

```
            }
    scr_rowcol(0,0);
    printf("    ");
    scr_rowcol(0,10);
    printf("type <any key> to continue <BRK> to end");
    c = ci();
    printf("\n");
            }
}

print(f,s,e,ans)
int s;
float d,e,ans;

{
    printf("YOUR SUM WAS --> %-8.8s  %c  %-8.8s = %-8.13s\n",no1,s,no2,ans);
    return;
}
clear()
{
    scr_clr();
    scr_rowcol(0,0);
    return;
}
mult(d,e)
float d,e;
{
    int s;
    float ans;
    ans = d * e;
    s = 88;
    print(d,e,s,ans);
    return;
}
divd(d,e)
float d,e;
{
    int s;
    float ans;
    ans = d \ e;
    s = 47,
    print(d,e,s,ans);
    return;
}
aded(d,e)
float d,e;
{
    int s;
    float ans;
```

```
        ans = d + e;
        s = 43;
        print(d,e,s,ans);
        return;
}
subt(d,e)
float d,e;
{
        int s;
        float ans;
        ans = d - e;
        s = 45;
        print(d,e,s,ans);
        return;
}
```

There are no new statements introduced in this program. Those previously introduced such as scanf() ci() and the screen handling routines are all used again. The main point of interest is the use of local variables. We have declared most of the variables that we will use inside function main(). This means that we cannot access these variables outside this function. If we wish to make use of the data that they contain we must pass their values as part of a function call. For example, to call the multiplication function and pass the values of variables d and e, we would use the following format:- mult(d,e); The value of variables d and e would then be passed to the function in question.

Since data is being passed to it the function must know how to deal with this incoming data. To enable it to do just this the data types of the variables passed must be declared before the main body of the function. Using function mult(d,e) as an example the following declarations are made:-

```
        mult(d,e)    /* function name and parameters passed */
        float d,e;   /* declares both parameters to be floating point  numbers */
        {            /* start of the main function body */
```

This type of parameter declaration has to be made for each of the functions in turn. With a large number of functions the extra overheads in programming time can become quite considerable.

There are some applications where the use of local variables can improve the general efficiency of a program, but as we have stated before we will tend to use global variables throughout the programs in this book.

Summary of Chapter 4.

(1)   Use of the #define command to simplify the entry of often used sections of code.

(2)   The #option FPLIB and #option INLIB commands to allow further commands and functions to be used in any C programs.

(3)   Further uses and full formatting syntax of the printf() statement.

(4)   Data manipulation commands, to allow the conversion of different data types. Those used were atof() and itof() and ftoa().

(5)   The introduction of single precision arithmetic operators to allow flexible handling of single precision numbers. The functions used were fmul(), fdiv, fsub and fadd.

(6)   The use of fgets() to allow flexible screen input of complex data items. This function inputs the data into a previously defined character array.

(7)   The introduction of nested function calls and function calls with parameter passing to allow flexible program construction with the minimum repetition of source code.

(8)   The introduction of some additional functions in the CP/M compiler. These allowed formatted input and the input of characters without screen echo.

Chapter 5

Files and Filing Methods.

Introduction to data files.

Whenever computers are used to store large amounts of data, they have to use some type of backing store. This is because the computer's internal memory is votatile (its contents are lost when the power is turned off) and the amount of data that can be stored in it is strictly limited. The two commonest types of backing store are magnetic tape and magnetic disk. Microcomputers in business applications use disks as their main backing store.

Data is stored on these disks in a data file. A file is simply a collection of related pieces of information, which are divided into records. For example, a payroll file could contain three records for each employee, one for the employee's name, the second for the employee's address and the third for the employee's works number. This type of file structure would be unusual and it would be far more common to have just one record for each employee and to have each record divided into fields (sub-divisions of a record). Generally, it is best to keep the file structure as simple as is possible. This helps the programmer when writing the program and also helps in future file maintenance.

Within each record the data is stored in fields. Returning to the payroll example each record would contain a surname field, a works number field and so on. The diagram in Figure 5.1 illustrates the breakdown.

Fixed and variable length records

The records within a file can be stored in one of two different ways. In fixed length records, each record is of the same length. This means that the various field lengths have to be decided in advance. The main advantage of this type of record is that it allows the computer to calculate the position of each physical record on the disk and then to access the data in any particular order. It would be possible to access record 56 immediately after record 78 and so on. The disadvantage of this method of data storage is that there can be a great deal of wasted space on the disk. This is because the fields each have to be as wide as the largest expected item of data. For example, with surnames the company may find that 298 employees have surnames of up to 8 characters but there is one person with a surname of 11 characters and one with 15. Then the whole surname field should really be a minimum of 15 characters long, although this would be excessive for most requirements.

Variable length records do not have a predetermined length allocated to them. They are therefore very economical of disk storage, but they have the disadvantage that they can only be accessed in sequence. This is because the computer can only place markers at the front and end of the file. If the 88th record had to be read then all the records 1-87 would have to be read first.

This illustrates one important aspect of computing, namely that an improvement in one area is often paid for by a loss of efficiency in another. This 'trade off' is found in many areas, particularly file handling.

Byte Stream Files

C does not have any facilities for dealing with direct or sequential access files. Any additional features that the programmer wishes to incorporate have to be written as a new function or functions. C treats files of data in a 'byte stream' fashion. This means that any data written onto the disk consists of a series of bytes of data which is not divided into fields or records. If the programmer wishes to so divide the file then external routines have to be used to do this.

Fig 5.1: A File, divided into records and fields

Record No.	Field 1 Surname	Field 2 Number	Field 3 Tax Code	Field 4 Salary	
1	ARBUTHNOT	10678	348	6025	
2	ASTON	21395	237	7500	
3	BAXTER	11224	423		
4	BRIGGS	10357	–		
5	BYLAND	49001			
6	CAPPER				File
7					

Methods of accessing files

There are four main methods of file access available to the computer user. These are as follows :-

(1) Byte stream access.
(2) Sequential access.
(3) Direct access.
(4) Indexed access.

As we have seen before, each of these methods will be expected to have advantages and disadvantages. The programmer has to decide which type of file access method is best suited to a particular task. Quite often a mixture of different accessing techniques is required. We will look at the four different types in order.

Byte Stream access

When accessing this type of file the program will simply read or write a continuous stream of bytes to or from the file specified by the programmer. There are two important files used as standard by C. These are the standard input file (keyboard) or stdin and the standard output file (screen) or stdout. The programmer is free to declare any of the physical devices (screen, keyboard, disk, printer) to be a file. We will deal with accessing each of these in turn as the need arises.

Sequential access

Sequential access files have their records stored on disk or tape in sequence. That is, the records are in the order that they were written. They are normally stored in variable length records although it is possible for them to be fixed length. A sequential access file has all the advantages and disadvantages of a variable length record file: it is a simple, compact and efficient type of file to construct, but it can be very slow to access as its length grows.

Direct access

Direct access files are often called Random Access files. Such files permit any record in the file to be accessed in just about the same length of time as any other. An analogy can be seen with a long playing record, in that any track can be selected equally rapidly, whereas on a cassette the whole tape must be wound through to find the 'track' you need.

Direct access files are composed of fixed length records and as such they have all the advantages and disadvantages of this type of record. Each record is written onto disk with an accompanying record number. This number is used to access the records, and so it is possible to read (say) record number 45 before any of the other records. It is also possible to access a record in such a file by means of a 'key'. This is a sequence of characters that is used to identify the record. For example, in a payroll file, the surname might be a suitable key. This key is used to access the record we need in one of two ways:

1. By using a 'look-up table' in which the keys are stored with their corresponding record numbers. Then, to find a particular record number, you (or the computer) scan through the keys until the required one is found, find its corresponding record number, and away you go.

2. By subjecting the key to some numerical transformation. This is called 'hashing' and is too big a subject to explain in detail here. Briefly, a possible transformation would be to assign a number to each character in the key (1 for A, 2 for B, etc), add all the numbers together, and square them to produce a 'pseudo-random' number. Then, the hashing scheme might divide this number by some other (usually a prime number) and find the remainder: the result is the record number required.

When constructing and using direct access files a certain amount of work has to be done to calculate the field lengths for the records. The main advantage of these files is that accessing them can be very fast and yet they can be accessed in sequence by using ascending record numbers. One of the main disadvantages of direct access files is that any records which have been deleted remain on the disk as blank records. If many deletions have occurred the file may have to be 'compressed' periodically to remove these blank records and to improve the files' storage efficiency.

Indexed files

These files are often called ISAM (Indexed Sequential Access Method) and are stored on disk in a completely sequential manner. In order to provide rapid access to any particular record, an index is maintained to subdivisions of the file. For example, if the ISAM file is ordered sequentially on the surname of workers listed on a payroll, a possible index could be:

Initial letter	Track	Sector
A	4	10
B	5	15
.	.	.
.	.	.
Z	15	12

The relationship between tracks and sectors is shown in Figure 7.2 . In order to find the record for a particular employee (e.g.JONES), we scan through the index until we find the entry for 'J' which might be track 10, sector 3. This tells us to go to track 10, sector 3, and begin our sequential search from there, until we find JONES. In this way, we have dramatically shortened the search time. Of course, this is a great oversimplification, and we do not mean to imply that this is how a real ISAM works in a real computer system, but it should give you the general idea.

ISAM files are similar to direct access files from the user's point of view, except that a record number is not the method of accessing the file. Instead, a key is used (see the above discussion of keys for random access files) and this can be any user defined string of characters. ISAM files consist of fixed length records and once again they have all their inherent advantages and disadvantages. They have a very similar speed of access to direct access files with the added benefit that if a deletion is made the record is removed from the file so no disk 'compaction' needs to be used. They do require more planning than direct access files due to the requirements of key maintenance and the number of records in the file.

Summary of accessing methods

Each of the three filing systems has advantages and disadvantages. Sequential files are quick and easy to build and maintain although they are very slow for most applications. Direct access files are quick and relatively easy to use but they can be rather inefficient in the use of disk storage space. Indexed files require rather more initial planning but are both quick and reasonably efficient in their use of disk space.

The choice of which filing system to use is up to the programmer. Each filing system has advantages and disadvantages and each is suited for a particular job. We can now look in detail to see how the C filing method works.

C is rather unusual in that it has no direct commands for dealing with relative or indexed files. What it does have is a very flexible approach to files. All input/output is done through files. As far as C is concerned even the screen and keyboard are files. It is possible to link the keyboard directly to a particular disk file or to the printer. Together with a number of other facilities that C offers, a very flexible range of file handling devices can be produced.

We will look at a simple file handling program that creates and maintains a disk file. This will then be extended to include a number of additional features, i.e. sorting, indexed filing systems, printer control and others. Our first program in this section is program 16 and this creates a disk file.

```
/* program 16 a file creator */

#include stdio/csh;
#option INLIB
#define fname "test/dat:1"
FILE *fp;
char a[30];
char b[30];
int c;
main()
{
  fp = fopen(fname,"w");
  c = 1;
  while( c != EOF)
  {
```

```
        clear();
        printf("NAME please --->:");
        fgets( &a[0],30,stdin );
        printf(" \n");
        printf("ADDRESS                            --");
        fgets( &b[0],30,stdin );
        printf(" \n");
        fputs( &a[0],fp);
        fputs( &b[0],fp);
        cursor(10,0);
        printf("type <any key> to continue <BRK> to end .\n");
        c = getchar();
    }
fclose(fp);
}

clear()
{
  fill(15360,1023,32);
  cursor(0,0);
}
```

This relatively simple program will form the basis for all of our disk-file programs. It simply creates a named disk file and then writes successive data items to it.

As usual it starts by stating the required include and option statements. In our case we will only be using the standard input/output functions and the INLIB option. The #define command states that the file name is "test/dat:1", this means that the file will be created with the name test/dat and be placed on drive number 1. (On CP/M systems the equivalent file name would be "b:test.dat"). The label used in the #define command is fname. Wherever this is used in the program the corresponding file name will be inserted.

The FILE *fp statement defines the pointer *fp to be a file pointer, and as such will be used to direct input/output to or from the file in question. Since we are only using one particular file we will only define one file pointer. The maximum number of files that can be accessed or opened at any one time is completely dependent on the compiler. Readers will have to consult the relevant manuals for details.

Two character arrays a and b are defined. These have a maximum space of 30 and due to the end of array marker, can only have 29 characters in each. The data will be entered into them using the fgets() command, as in our calculator example. Only one integer variable is declared, this is c and will be used for our usual key responses.

There are two program functions in the program. One of these is our standard screen clear function, clear(). We have looked at this in detail and it will not be commented on again. The other function is main() and this contains the program body.

Main() starts with a file open statement. The general syntax for this is:-

```
fp = fopen(fname,"abc");
```

Where fp is a valid file pointer (defined above), fname is a valid file name (dependent on the operating system) and "abc" is one of the standard modes. These may be "r" ("R") to read the file, "w" ("W") to write to the file or "a" ("A") to append data to the file.

In our example the file is opened in append mode. This means that the file will be created if it does not exist and data will be written to it without overwriting any existing data. Had we declared the file as open mode "w" then any data already on the file would be destroyed when we wrote new data onto it. Any file that is opened for both input and output by two or more calls to fopen() will behave in a completely unpredictable way. This should not be done. If a file's usage changes in a program the file must be closed and then reopened. We will look at this in a later example.

The next two commands set the value of variable c and carry out the test part of the while..... loop. The body of the loop clears the screen and accepts the two data items. The data is accepted by the fgets() commands. Two printf() statements are included to produce screen prompts. The new line characters are printed after the data has been accepted to make the screen echo of the data appear immediately after the prompts.

The next command is another new file command, it is fputs() and its syntax is shown below:-

```
retcode = fputs( string, fp );
```

In this command string is a pointer to a character array, or to a string of characters, fp is a file pointer (defined above). Our examples are :-

```
fputs( &a[0],fp );
fputs( &b[0],fp );
```

In each case the relevant array is output to the file specified by fp. The effect of this is that the file "test/dat:1" will have the contents of arrays 'a' and 'b' written to it.

The retcode part of the fputs() command gives us a way of testing whether the fputs() statement has been executed correctly or not. If retcode is equal to zero then no error has occurred. If an error has been detected then retcode will be set to EOF (-1). In the fopen() command the file pointer (fp) is set to zero if an error has occurred. It is possible to use this to test the validity of the fopen statement. The use of these testing values is important in large systems applications and they will only be used in some of our larger filing programs.

The final lines of the program print out the message and then accepts the user's response into variable c. If the response is <BRK> or <CTRL-C> the command fclose(fp); is carried out. This closes the file declared by fp.

```
/* program 16 CP/M a file creator */

#define stdin 0
#define stdout 1
#define fname "b:test.dat"
char a[30];
char b[30];
int fp,c;
main()
{
  fp = fopen(fname,"a");
  c = 1;
  while( c != EOF)
  {
    clear();
    printf("NAME please --->:");
    fgets( &a[0],30,stdin );
    printf(" \n");
    printf("ADDRESS                              --");
    fgets( &b[0],30,stdin );
    printf(" \n");
    fputs( &a[0],fp);
    fputc( 0x0a,fp );
    fputs( &b[0],fp);
    fputc( 0x0a,fp );
    scr_rowcol(0,10);
    printf("type <any key> to continue <CTRL-C> to end . \n");
    c = ci();
  }
fclose(fp);
}

clear()
{
  scr_clr();
  scr_rowcol(0,0);
}
```

The CP/M version of our file create program has a few modifications. Apart from the usual #define differences there is one important change. In the CP/M compiler the fgets() function does not return either a CR (carriage return) character or a LF (line feed) one. Since any file read program will look for one of these we must include a specific command to place one of these characters onto the file, after any disk write statement. In program 16 CP/M this is done by means of an fputc(0x0a, fp) command which simply places a line feed character (hexadecimal 0a) in with the file.

The other important difference is in the way that the CP/M compiler handles the file pointer. With LC we had to declare a file pointer by means of the command

FILE *fp. The DeSmet compiler declares an integer variable (i.e. fp) and this is used by the command fp = fopen(fname,"a");. The principle is similar. In one a file pointer is used to store the return code,in the other an integer variable is used. Otherwise the two sets of file commands function in the same way.

So far we have only created a file and written same data onto it. This is useful, but rather pointless unless we are able to read the information from the disk. Our next program enables us to do just this. It is a very short program and is designed to demonstrate the methods that will be developed in later chapters. Program 17 as stated is simply a file read program, the listing appears below:-

```
/* Program 17 read a disk file */;

#include stdio/csh
#option INLIB
int c;
FILE *fp;
main()
{
  fill(15360,1024,0);
  cursor(0,0);
  fp = fopen("test/dat:1","r");
  while (( c = getc(fp)) != EOF)
  putc(c,stdout);
  fclose(fp);
}
```

This program is similar in structure to our file create program. The usual options are included and the file pointer is the same. There is only one program function, main(). This starts with the clear screen and cursor reset commands. The reason that we have not put these in a separate function is that we will only use the commands once and therefore it is not really practical to use a function definition.

The file pointer (fp) is then declared fopen() with the file as named in program 16. The mode used in this program is "r" since we are only interested in reading the file.

The while..... loop is a little different to our usual command. It is still in the same general format but the command inside the test part is different. This uses the getc() command as opposed to the getchar() statement. The reason for this is that the getc() statement allows us to define the file that we wish to use. The getchar() command only uses the standard input file (usually the keyboard). Otherwise the commands are similar. Both return the integer representation of the character. The general syntax of the command is:-

$$c = getc(fp);$$

Where c is an integer and fp is a relevant file pointer.

The while... loop tests the character just read and if it is not equal to the end of file character then it is output to the screen (standard output). This is done by the use of the putc(); statement. This is very similar to the getc() command but is used for output of a character. The syntax is:-

$$cret = putc(c, fp);$$

Where c is the character to be output and fp is a relevant file pointer. The return code (cret) is set equal to the character output if the output is successful. If not, then the two will be different.

The file pointer in this point is stdout, which is the standard output (the screen). When the end of file character is read the file is closed and the program ends.

```
/* Program 17 CP/Mread a disk file */;

#define stdout 1
#define EOF -1
int c, fp;
main()
{
  scr-clr();
  scr-rowcol(0,0);
  fp = fopen("b:test.dat","r");
  while (( c = getc(fp)) != EOF)
  putc(c,stdout);
  fclose(fp);
}
```

The CP/M version of program 17 is very similar to the LC listing. The only point worth commenting on is the fact that the EOF definition is now -1 rather than the value 3 that we have used previously. The reason for this is that in our other examples the value of 3 was used to test for the <CTRL-C> key. This returned a value of 3 from the keyboard, hence the definition of EOF. Now that we are dealing with file input the test condition has to be against -1, the value returned when the end of a disk file is encountered. These differences are really a result of the differences between the different operating systems.

Now that we have seen how to create and read a file we are in a position to be able to search the file for information. Unfortunately, the fact that C only uses a byte stream file structure will slow down our search technique. We can get over this by some advanced programming techniques which will be dealt with later in the book. For now we will content ourselves with a simple sequential search method.

Program 18 is the one that deals with the searching of the file. As can be seen, the program is somewhat longer than the previous two. This is due to the fact that the basic structure of a searching program is going to be more complex than either a simple write-to-disk or a read-from-disk program. Apart from anything else, we have to allow for the fact that one of two possible outcomes may result. (1) the data searched for is found (2) the data searched for is not found.

The listing for program 18 is shown below:-

```
/* program 18 search the file */

#define fname "test/dat:1"
#define space printf("\n \n")
FILE *fp;
char a[30];
char b[30];
char d[30];
int c,err;
main()
{
  while( c != EOF)
  {
    fp = fopen(fname,"r");
    clear();
    printf("Please enter the NAME you want -->:");
    fgets(&d[0],30,stdin);
    printf(" \n");
    do
      {
        err = fgets( &a[0],30,fp);
        fgets( &b[0],30,fp);
      }
    while( strcmp( &a[0], &d[0] ) != 0 && err != 0);
    clear();
    if( err != 0 )
    {
      printf("The data that you required is :" );
      printf(" \n");
      fputs( &a[0],stdout);
      fputs( &b[0],stdout);
      space;
    }
    else
    if( err == 0 )
      {
      printf("Sorry the name that you entered was not in the file \n");
      space;
    printf("Press <BREAK> to finish, any other key to continue the search\n");
    fclose(fp);
    c = getchar();
  }
}
clear()
```

```
{
    fill(15360,1023,32);
    cursor(0,0);
}
```

Program 18 starts in the usual way, we have the #options that we require and the definitions of the character arrays. There are three arrays, one for the data that we are searching for, the other two to contain the data read from the disk file. The file name is declared and also a space label which will be used to print two line feeds, the next declaration is the file pointer *fp. Two integers are declared, c and err. The purpose of c is as before, err is going to be used to detect an error during a file read operation.

There are two program functions, (1) main() which contains the program body and (2) clear() which contains the screen clear commands.

Function main() starts with a while.... loop. This allows the file to be repeatedly searched for a particular string of data that will be entered by the user. The file pointer fp is set to the relevant disk file and the fopen() mode is set to "r" (since we are interested in reading the file). A clear screen call is then made which is followed by the prompt to enter the data that will be searched for. The screen print of the message and the method of accepting the reply into array 'd' is exactly the same as in previous examples.

Once the required data has been entered a new line (linefeed) is printed onto the screen and a do......while loop is entered. The reason for the do....while loop instead of a while... loop is that it enables us to execute the body of the loop once before the relevant tests are made. There are,as ever, a number of other ways in which the same procedure could be carried out but we will use this one.

The do....while loop is somewhat complex and will require a detailed explanation. It is printed below to assist in the explanation.

```
do
  {
    err = fgets( &a[0],30,fp);
    fgets( &b[0],30,fp);
  }
while( strcmp( &a[0], &d[0] ) !=0 && err !=0);
```

The statements

```
err = fgets( &a[0],30,fp);
fgets( &b[0],30,fp);
```

are carried out once. The first of these reads in the first part of the data in the file. (remember the data is in two parts, the name and then the address). If some error occurs i.e. no data or the end of the file then err is set to zero. The second statement reads the second part of the data pair (the address).

65

The test part of the loop is contained in the while() statement.

This states

$$\text{while(strcmp(\&a[0], \&d[0]) != 0 \&\& err != 0);}$$

and tests for the two conditions

(1)   strcmp(&a[0], &d[0]) !=0

and

(2)   err !=0

Condition number (1) is a function contained in the INLIB library of functions. It is a sophisticated function that compares the two strings within the brackets. A code of zero is returned if the strings are equal. So the statement as written tests if the two strings are equal. Condition number (2) simply tests to see if variable err is equal to zero. The loop will be repeatedly executed while the two strings are not equal and no error is encountered during the fgets() operation. If either of these two conditions is met then execution of the loop is terminated.

The do....while loop then repeatedly reads the two data items until a match is found or an error is encountered. Normally the only error that would be encountered is the program trying to read the end of the file.

The loop is terminated in one of two possible states. If err is equal to zero then the end of the file has been reached without the string being found. If err is not equal to zero then the string was found. The remainder of the program uses the state of err to determine the course of action.

Once the do...while loop is exited the screen is cleared and an if...then...else construct is entered. The first condition that is tested for is the if(err != 0) one. If this is true (err is not equal to zero) then the two strings are equal i.e. the string searched for has been found and the statements within the braces are executed. These print out the message onto the screen and then the two data items are printed onto the screen using the fputs() commands. The use of the fputs() command has been explained earlier and will not be discussed further. Once the data has been output to the screen the space label forces two linefeeds and the if...then....else command is exited.

Should the if(err != 0) be untrue (err is equal to zero) then the end of the file was reached before the two strings were found to be equal. In this case the else... part of the statement is executed and the message "Sorry the name that you entered was not in the file " is printed.

The final part of the program prints out the usual continuation message and then waits for the user's response. Before the user's response the file is closed. This serves two purposes. If the user has finished with the program then the file needs to be closed. If, however, the user wishes to continue and search for another data item then the file will have to be closed, then reopened to allow the data search to start from the beginning of the file.

If the user types <BRK> or <CTRL-C> then the program terminates.

```
/* program 18 CP/M search the file */

#define fname "b:test.dat"
#define space printf("\n \n")
#define EOF 3
#define stdin 0
#define stdout 1
int fp,sl,c,err;
char a[30];
char b[30];
char d[30];
main()
{
  while( c != EOF)
  {
    fp = fopen(fname,"r");
    clear();
    _setmem(&d[0],30,0);
    printf("Please enter the NAME you want -->:");
    fgets( &d[0],30,stdin );
    sl = strlen(&d[0]);
    d[sl] = 0x0a;
    printf("\n");
    do
      {
        err = fgets( &a[0],30,fp);
        fgets( &b[0],30,fp);
      }
    while( strcmp( &a[0], &d[0] ) != 0 && err != 0);
    clear();
    if( err != 0 )
    {
      printf("The data that you required is :" );
      printf(" \n");
      fputs( &a[0],stdout);
      fputs( &b[0],stdout);
      space;
    }
    else
    if( err == 0 )
    {
      printf("Sorry the name that you entered was not in the file \n");
      space;
```

```
    }
    printf("Press <CTRL-C> to finish, any other key to continue the search \n");
    fclose(fp);
    c = ci();
  }
}
clear()
{
  scr_clr();
  scr_rowcol(0,0);
}
```

When looking at the DeSmet compiler listing, the first point to note is the similarity of almost all of the main sections of code. Apart from one or two code lines the two programs are identical. This further illustrates the point that the C language is relatively standard, compared to a language like BASIC.

The main difference in the two programs deals with the problem of the fgets() function that was mentioned before. We use this function to load the array d with the data that will be used for the search routine. Since fgets() does not automatically place an LF character at the end of the array and we have one at the end of each block of data in the file, the two will never match in the compare routine. To overcome this we place a hexadecimal 0a at the end of the data entered by the user. This corrects the first problem but generates a more subtle one. Since our data now has a LF character in it, if we enter a shorter string of data in our next iteration of the search routine the data string will then have two LF characters and once again no match will occur. We will have to correct this by clearing the array (by filling it with hexadecimal blanks 0x00) before we use the fgets() function. The sequence of events is outlined below:-

      (1)   clear the array.
      (2)   enter the data.
      (3)   calculate the string length.
      (4)   place the LF character in string position d[string length].

The reason that the LF character is placed at the data array element indicated by string length is that the value of the string length gives the overall length of the string, but the array elements are numbered from element 0. Element (string length) will therefore be the last plus one element in the array. The four lines of code that correspond to these actions are as follows:-

```
_setmem( &d[0],30,0 );
fgets(&d[0],30,stdin);
sl = strlen(&d[0]);
d[sl] = 0x0a;
```

In the DeSmet compiler the _setmem() function works in the same way as the fill() function of the LC compiler. Apart from this modification to the program, the remainder functions in exactly the same way as the LC program listing.

Our final program in this chapter covers the use of files together with the creation of a menu. This is a commonly used technique in computing and its purpose is to present the user with a number of options. By selecting the required option (usually done by pressing an appropriate key) the required function is evoked. The listing for this program is shown in program 19.

```
/* Program 19 a menu driven filing system */

#include stdio/csh;
#option INLIB
#define space printf("\n\n")
FILE *fp;
char a[31];
char b[31];
char d[31];
char e[16];
char *cp;
int c,c1,c2,c3,sel,err;


main()
{
    c = c1 = c2 = c3 = 1;
    while(c1 != EOF)

    {
    clear();
    cursor(10,2);
    printf("TYPE <R> TO READ THE FILE \n");
    cursor(10,4);
    printf("TYPE <W> TO WRITE TO THE FILE \n");
    cursor(10,6);
    printf("TYPE <X> TO EXIT THE PROGRAM  \n");
    c1= getchar();
      if(c1==114)read();
        else
          if(c1==119)write();
            else
              if(c1==120)exit(0);
                else
                  continue;

}
    exit(0);
}


read()
```

```c
{
  sel = 0;
  file_name();
  c = 0;
  while( c != 120 )
    {
    fp = fopen(cp,"r");
    if(fp == NULL)
      {
        sel = 2;
        err_trp();
      }
    clear();
    cursor(5,2);
    printf("Please enter the NAME you want -->:");
    fgets( &d[0],30,stdin );
    printf(" \n");
    do
      {
      err = fgets( &a[0],30,fp);
      fgets( &b[0],30,fp);
      }
    while( strcmp( &a[0], &d[0] ) != 0 && err != 0);
    clear();
    if( err != 0 )
      {
      printf("The data that you required is :" );
      printf(" \n");
      fputs( &a[0],stdout);
      fputs( &b[0],stdout);
      space;
      }
    else
    if( err == 0 )
      {
      printf("Sorry the name that you entered was not in the file \n");
      space;
      }
    fclose(fp);
    mesg();
    c = getchar();
    if(c == EOF) exit(0);
}
  return;
}


write()
{
```

```c
    sel = 0;
    file_name();
    fp = fopen(cp,"a");
    if(fp == NULL)
        {
          sel = 1;
          err_trp();
        }
    c2 = 0;
    while( c2 != 120 )
    {
    clear();
    cursor(5,2);
    printf("NAME please --->:");
    fgets( &a[0],30,stdin );
    printf(" \n");
    cursor(5,4);
    printf("ADDRESS   ----->:");
    fgets( &b[0],30,stdin );
    printf(" \n");
    fputs( &a[0],fp);
    fputs( &b[0],fp);
    mesg();
    c2 = getchar();
    if(c2 == EOF )exit(0);
}
    fclose(fp);
return;
}


clear()
{
    fill(15360,1023,32);
    cursor(0,0);
}
mesg()
{
    cursor(10,15);
    printf("TYPE <X> TO END any other key to continue ");
}
file_name()
{
    cp = &e[0];
    clear();
    printf("Please enter the name of the file \n");
    fgets( cp,15,stdin);
}

key()
```

```
{
   c3 = getchar();
}

err_trp()
}
if(fp == NULL)
   {
     clear();
     cursor(0,12);
     if(sel==1)
       {
         printf("ERROR !!!! UNABLE TO OPEN FILE \n");
       }
     else
       if(sel == 2)
         {
            printf("ERROR !!!! FILE DOES NOT EXIST \n");
       }
     printf("type <C> to continue <E> to end. ");
     key();
       if(c3 == 'c' ) main();
         else
         if(c3 == 'e' || c3 == EOF) exit(0);
           else
             if( c3 != 'c' && c3 != 'e') err-trp();
   }
   }
```

The program has the usual first section. The main differences being the definition of 'space' to mean two linefeeds, a file pointer *fp, a character pointer *cp, four arrays, and a number of integer variables.

There are eight program functions in all. These range from the very simple key() to the more complex errtrp(). We will look at each function in turn.

Our first function is main() and this contains the main program body. In it the variables c,c_1,c_2,c_3 are all set equal to 1. This is done by means of the line $c = c_1 = c_2 = c_3 = 1$, and this serves to set each variable successively equal to 1. The function is primarily concerned with presenting the user with the menu selection, accepting the response and causing program control to be diverted to the relevant section of the program. To this end there is a while...... loop which clears the screen, resets the cursor and then presents the user with three messages namely, to read a file, to write to a file or to exit the program. These are presented in the usual way with the printf() command. Variable c_1 is then set equal to the user's response by using the c_1 = getchar() command. A nested if....else construct follows which repeatedly tests the value of c_1 and if it is equal to any of the preset values the corresponding function call is envoked.

For example, if the user presses key 'w' then the second branch of the test would be evaluated 'true' and function write() would be called. This is because the user's key response is stored as an integer value of 119 and the test condition if(c1 == 119)write(); would be evaluated as true.

The purpose of the continue; statement after the last else is to enable the programmer to see that the while.... loop will reiterate if a key other than 'x' or 'r' or 'w' is pressed. This command could have been missed out but it serves to draw our attention to the fact that the loop is terminating at this point.

The read function is the next one in the listing. As its name suggests, it is responsible for reading the file. It starts by setting variable sel to zero. This is followed by a call to function file name() which prompts the user to enter the file name. (we will look at this function a little later). After this variable c is set to zero and a while... loop is begun.

The first statement in the while.... loop opens the file using pointer cp to point to the file name (entered using function file name). this is opened in 'read mode' as we would expect. Remembering back to what was said about the return codes of various function calls we will see how these can be used. Our file open call returns a value of NULL in fp if an error exists. In this case the main source of error would be that the file does not exist. Following the fopen() call there is an if... test which tests to see if fp has been set to NULL. If it has then variable sel is set to 2 and the error trapping function err trp() is called. It can be seen that this function makes use of the value of sel which is available to it since sel is a global variable. If the value of fp is not NULL then this branch of the program is not executed.

The next statement in the body of function read() clears the screen and then prompts the user for the name to be read from the file. (as in our previous examples the data stored on the file consists of names and addresses. The required name is entered by the use of the fgets() function and is read into array d from the keyboard.

A do....while loop is now executed. This is used to force one execution of the statements before the exit test is carried out. In our loop the two statements :-

```
err = fgets( &a[0],30,fp);
fgets( &b[0],30,fp);
```

are carried out. These read in the values of the name and the address into the arrays a and b. The file that is to be read is set by the pointer fp. Once the first read has occurred the while(); test is carried out. This states:-

```
while( strcmp( &a[0], &d[0] ) != 0 && err != 0);
```

which means that the do... loop will continue until one of the two conditions in the above is evaluated as being true. The two conditions are

(1) the two arrays a and d are equal.
(2) the variable err is equal to 0.

Condition (1) will occur if the value of strcmp() is equal to zero. This will only be when the data contained in arrays a and d are equal. The function strcmp() actually compares the two arrays and returns a value depending on whether array a is less than, greater than or equal to array d. In our example we are only interested in the situation where the two arrays are equal. (for further information on the use of strcmp() the user should consult the relevant manual).

Condition (2) occurs when there has been an error in the file read operation. This will most usually be when the end of the file has been encountered. When the end of the file has been reached the value of variable err is zero. Should this condition exist then it means that the file has been read and the data searched for has not been found. Otherwise the program would have terminated this loop at the point where strcmp() was equal to zero.

The next command is an if.... test that checks to see if variable err is equal to zero. If it is not (i.e. the required data has been found) then the following five statements are executed. These print out a heading, a new line, the data and two new lines (defined by space);

If variable err is equal to zero (i.e. the file has been read and the data not found) then the else part of the if... test is carried out. This simply prints out the message that the data was not found during the read.

The file is then closed and function mesg() executed. This is another simple function that prints out a message to the user. The user's response is assigned to variable c and if this is equal to EOF (the <BRK> or <CTRL-C> keys) the program is terminated. By pressing the 'x' key the user is returned to the main menu. This is carried out by the use of the outermost while.... loop. (while(c != 120); 120 being the integer representation of the character 'x'). Any other key reopens the file and the process continues.

It is necessary to close and then re-open the file since we only have a byte stream file, and as such the only way of returning to the beginning of this file is by closing and then opening the file in question.

The final function that directly deals with the filing process is the write() function. There are similarities to the read() function in the way that various file operations are carried out.

At the start of the function the variable sel is set to zero and the function file_name() is called. This returns the file name of the file to be read. The pointer cp is used to direct the fp = fopen(cp, "a") command to the start of the file name. The mode used in this fopen() command is "a", which means that if the file does not exist then it will be created, if it does exist the file pointer (an imaginary pointer to the position of different records in the file) will be set to the end of the file. Any further data written to the file will then be added onto the end of the existing file. As a result of this it is possible to add data to the file on a number of separate occasions. Using the "w" mode any existing data would be overwritten each time a new write operation was carried out.

Should any errors occur when the fopen() call is made, then the variable fp is set to NULL. This value is tested for in the next statement if(fp == NULL). If fp has the value NULL then an error has occurred and the two commands within the body of the if... statement are executed. These set variable sel to one and then pass this value to function err_trp().

If the file open has been successful then variable c2 is set to zero and the next while.... loop is carried out. The main purpose of this loop is to accept the names and addresses (that represent the data items) and write them to disk.

The screen is cleared in the usual way, and the prompts and cursor commands function in the same ways as before. There is a very large range of possible screen presentations possible here and the individual user could vary this part of the program without very much difficulty.

The final few lines of this function get the user's response to the screen message mesg(), and if it is 'x' the file is closed and the program returns to the main menu. Pressing <BRK> or <CTRL-C> causes the program to terminate.

There are five final functions in the filing program. Three of these have either been looked at before or are sufficiently brief as to be self explanatory. We will concentrate on the two main functions in this section.

The first of these is the function file name() which is the function that obtains the name of the file from the user. At the start of this function the pointer cp is set to the start of the array e by means of the cp = &e[0] command. The screen is then cleared and the message printed. The function fgets() then reads in the user's response from the keyboard. A string of up to fourteen characters can be entered here. Once entered the function returns to the calling function with cp pointing to the file name.

Our final function is err_trp(). This is a function to print out a particular screen message, depending on the state of variable sel. The value of sel will be set according to which part of the main program a fault occurred in. In our relatively simple program there are two possible places where a fault could have occurred. The first is in the read section and the second is in the write section. Variable sel would then be set to either two or one respectively.

As a reflection of this there are two test sections in this function. The first message is printed out if sel is equal to one. Otherwise the second message is printed onto the screen. Finally a prompt is displayed which guides the user onto the next stage of the program. Two possible key responses are made here. If 'c' is pressed then control is passed back to main(), if 'e' is pressed then the program terminates. Should the user type some other key then the function calls itself and waits for a correct key press to occur. This is done by means of the statement

if(c3 != 'c' && c3 != 'e') err_trp(sel);

which performs the function err_trp() if both of the conditions contained in the above expression are found to be true. This type of function call, where a function calls itself is called recursion. It is a feature of some of the more modern languages that they are able to do this.


```
/* Program 19 CP/M a menu driven filing system */

#define EOF 3
#define stdin 0
#define stdout 1
#define space printf(" \n\n")
#define NULL 0
char a[31];
char b[31];
char d[31];
char e[16];
char *cp;
int sl,fp,c,c1,c2,c3,sel,err;

main()
{
   c = c1 = c2 = c3 =1;
   while(c1 != EOF)

  {
   clear();
   scr_rowcol(2,10);
   printf("TYPE <R> TO READ THE FILE \n");
   scr_rowcol(4,10);
   printf("TYPE <W> TO WRITE TO THE FILE \n");
   scr rowcol(6,10);
   printf("TYPE <X> TO EXIT THE PROGRAM \n");
   c1= ci();
     if(c1==114)readn();
       else
         if(c1==119)writen();
           else
             if(c1==120)exit(0);
               else
                 continue;
}
  exit(0);
}


readn()
{
  sel = 0;
  file_name();
```

76

```c
c = 0;
while( c != 120 )
{
  fp = fopen(cp,"r");
  if(fp == NULL)
    {
        sel = 2;
        err_trp();
    }
  clear();
  _setmem(&d[0],31,0);
  scr_rowcol(5,2);
  printf("Please enter the NAME you want -->:");
  fgets( &d[0],30,stdin );
  sl = strlen(&d[0]);
  d[sl] = 0x0a;
  printf(" \n");
  do
  {
    err = fgets( &a[0],30,fp);
    fgets( &b[0],30,fp);
  }
  while( strcmp( &a[0], &d[0] ) != 0 && err != 0);
  clear();
  if( err != 0 )
  {
    printf("The data that you required is :" );
    printf(" \n");
    fputs( &a[0],stdout);
    fputs( &b[0],stdout);
    space;
  }
  else
  if( err == 0 )
  {
    printf("Sorry the name that you entered was not in the file\n");
    space;
    }
  fclose(fp);
  mesg();
  c = ci();
  if(c == EOF) exit(0);
}
  return;
}


writen()
{
```

```c
      sel = 0;
      file_name();
      fp = topen(cp,"a");
      if(fp == NULL)
        {
          sel = 1;
          err_trp();
        }
      c2 = 0;
      while( c2 != 120 )
        {
      clear();
      scr_rowcol(2,5);
      printf("NAME please --->:");
      fgets( &a[0],30,stdin );
      printf(" \n");
      scr_rowcol(4,5);
      printf("ADDRESS ----->:"); ·
      fgets( &b[0],30,stdn );
      printf(" \n");
      fputs( &a[0],fp);
      fputc( 0x0a,fp );
      fputs( &b[0],fp);
      fputc( 0x0a,fp );
      mesg();
      c2 = ci();
      if(c2 == EOF )exit(0);
}
      fclose(fp);
      return;
}


clear()
{
  scr_clr();
  scr_rowcol(0,0);
}
mesg()
{
  scr_rowcol(15,10);
  printf("TYPE <X> TO END any other key to continue ");
}

file_name()
{
      _setmem( &e[0],31,0 );
      cp = &e[0];
      clear();
```

```
        printf("Please enter the name of the file \n");
        fgets( cp,15,stdin);
        sl = strlen( &e[0] );
        e[0] = 0x0a;

}

key()
{
    c3 = ci();
}

err_trp()
{
if(fp == NULL)
    {
        clear();
        scr_rowcol(12,0);
        if(sel==1)
            {
            printf("ERROR !!!! UNABLE TO OPEN FILE \n");
            }
          else
            if(sel == 2)
                {
                printf("ERROR !!!! FILE DOES NOT EXIST \n");
                }
        printf("type <C> to continue <E> to end. ");
        key();
        if(c3 == 'c' ) main();
            else
            if(c3 == 'e' || c3 == EOF) exit(0);
                else
                if( c3 != 'c' && c3 != 'e') err_trp();
    }
    }
```

The DeSmet program listing is very similar to the LC program. Almost all of the differences have been explained before and so most will not be repeated. This applies to the #define statements, the problems with the fgets() function, the clear() differences and so on. The only point worth mentioning is that the read() and write() functions have been renamed readn() and writen() respectively. This is due to the fact that there are two functions read() and write() supplied as standard in the DeSmet C compiler. These deal with other aspects of file input/output and so we have renamed our functions.

Summary of chapter 5.

(1) The use of data files and the different types of such files.

(2) The fopen() function and the different modes available for use with it.

(3) The concept of opening a data file and writing a stream of data to it.

(4) Reading data from the file using the fgets() function and a new file pointer.

(5) Searching the file for information. The use of the strcmp() function to compare two strings of data.

(6) Creating a 'menu driven' filing program, incorporating all of the above techniques.

(7) The use of return codes and error codes to obtain information about the success or failure of a particular operation.

(8) The construction of separate routines to process these 'error conditions'.

Chapter 6

Printed output and Printer drivers.

This chapter deals with printers and the construction of printer drivers. Quite simply, a printer driver is a short program which controls the output to a printer.

C deals with printers by considering them to be the same as any other file. This is quite consistent with the way in which C handles all input and output. To obtain access to the printer a relevant file has to be declared and opened in mode "w". Any output will then be sent to the file in question.

Our first program, program 20, directs output to the printer. It also acts as a very simple printer driver. The reason why this is necessary is that the text-editor (a simple word processor) that was used to produce some sections of this book, stores the data on disk as a continuous stream of characters. If a paragraph consisted of 3000 words then these would be stored as a string of 3000 words with no -end of line- markers. When this is printed the printer treats the data as if it were a continuous stream of text and does not make any attempt to tidy the output. As a result of this the text appears as a full 80 characters per line (depending on the printer) but with the words split at the 80th character with no regards for word endings. The text is printed but in a very untidy form.

We will illustrate the way in which C can be used to write a printer driver by starting with a very simple method and developing it to be a full variable-format printer driver.

```
/* Program 20 a simple printer driver */

#include stdio/csh;
#define hard "*pr"
int err,i,ch;
FILE *fp, *ff;

main()
{
```

```
fp = fopen("chpt1c/pcl:1","r");
ff = fopen(hard,"w");
i=1;
ch = 1;
err= 0x0d;
while( (ch = getc(fp))!= EOF)
   {
     if(( i >= 60 ) && (ch == 0x20))
        {
          putc(err,ff); i=1;
        }
     else
        putc(ch,ff);
     putchar(ch);
     if(ch!=0x0d)++i;
        else
           i = 1;

   }
fclose();
}
```

Our program begins as before by stating the library files that will be included in the program and declaring all the variables, etc that will be used. We define the character string 'hard' to be equivalent to *pr. This is the same as our other definitions except that *pr is an operating system device meaning the printer. It can be considered to be much the same as a pointer, by opening a file to *pr we actually open a file to the printer.

Three integer variables are used and two file pointers are declared.

There is only one function in this program. It begins by opening two files. One is a disk file (chpt1c/pcl:1) which is the first chapter of the book on drive one. Since we are only interested in copying this chapter to the printer we have opened the file in "r" mode. Our second file is the printer file. The full statement is ff = (*pr, "w"); using the relevant substitution from 'hard'. Any output directed to pointer ff will now go to the printer.

The next three statements in this piece of program initialise the variables, and prevent any problems with these variables having randomised values before the main program begins.

Before we consider what the next pieces of program are going to do we must consider exactly what we want our printer driver to accomplish.

The main problem that we want to overcome is the fact that the printer does not recognise the end of a word, when it comes near the end of a line. On most micro-computer printers the standard column width is eighty columns. We will assume that no word is going to be longer than twenty characters. With this assumption we can start looking at the data stream being read from the disk file and check to see if a word has ended (i.e. a space occurs). If this is so and we are at a column position greater than or equal to sixty, then the printer driver will generate a new line.

Once a new line has been produced the column counter is set back to one and the process starts again. In this way our printer driver simply generates a new line each time a word ends after column sixty. We could quite easily have used a column position of seventy to generate a new line, but this places us at risk from words over ten characters in length. In such a situation our driver would split the word across lines, as before.

Variable err is set to the new line character (hexadecimal 0d) and will be printed each time a new line is required.

The main part of the program consists of a while.... loop which reads the disk data file in question and checks to see if the character is an end of file marker. If it is, then the process terminates.

The first statement inside the while.... loop is the if() one. This checks to see if the variable ch (containing the value of the data item just read from disk) meets both of our two test conditions. (Is the column number greater than or equal to sixty and is the character equal to a space ?). If these conditions are met then the body of the if.. statement is executed.

The statement in the body of the if... test simply outputs the character contained in variable err to the file pointed to by ff. In our case this is the printer. Once this has been done the column position counter, variable i, is reset to 1 (indicating that a new line has just been started).

If the two conditions above have not been met then the statement after the else.... part are carried out. In program 20 this consists of only one line put(ch,ff) which simply outputs the character to the printer. The statement that follows this prints the character to the screen (it echoes the printer output to the screen). It will always do this since it is not part of a compound statement after the else.... part of the test.

The next group of statements are a number of checks, structured as an if...else statement.

The reason for these is that we have not allowed for all of the possiblities that could exist in the incoming text. The text could have contained some end of line markers at, say, the end of a paragraph and the end of a table. If these are treated as an ordinary character the column counter would continue counting up although a new line had been generated to the printer.

The first if....else loop tests to see if ch contained the value (hexadecimal 0d) if it did not then the column counter (i) is incremented. If ch did represent a new line then the value of i is reset to one.

When the while.... loop is executed an fclose() statement is carried out. This closes the files and the program terminates.

```
/* Program 20 CP/M a simple printer driver */

#define EOF -1
#define hard "LST:"
int err,err1,i,ch,fp,ff;

main()
{
  fp = fopen("b:chpt1c.pcl","r");
  ff = fopen(hard,"w");
  i=1;
  ch = 1;
  err= 0x0d;
  err1 = 0x0a;
  while( (ch = getc(fp))!= EOF)
     {
      if(( i >= 60 ) && (ch == 0x20))
         {
             putc(err,ff);
             putc(err1,ff);
             i = 1;
         }
        else
           putc(ch,ff);
        putchar(ch);
        if(ch!=0x0d)++i;
              else
                 i = 1;
  }
fclose();
}
```

The CP/M version of the printer driver contains a few interesting variations. The first is that the method of defining the printer is different. Our program uses a #define hard "LST:" statement. In this CP/M system the LST device is usually the parallel output. If output had to go to the serial port the command would have been #define hard "TTY:". Whenever a file is opened with the name 'hard' then any future output will be sent to the parallel port.

We have used two err variables, (err and err1). The reason for this is that the printer does not add a LF after a CR (line feed after a carriage return). By defining the variables err and err1 to be 0x0d and 0x0a respectively, we can output the required control characters whenever they are needed.

Apart from these changes, the only program modifications are to output the LF character after a CR has been printed. This can be seen in the pair of statements:-

```
putc(err,ff);
putc(err1,ff);
```

There is only one other place in the program where this technique might be required. This is in the section:-

```
else
    putc(ch,ff);
```

In this piece of code no LF is sent after a CR character. The reason for this is that the data is stored on disk in such a way that for every CR character written to disk there is an accompanying LF. This means that the program will 'self adjust' at this point. Any further adjustment on our part would cause a double spaced line.

While program 20 produces an acceptable, if rather ragged, output our printer driver would be a much better utility if it contained some additional features. Firstly we would rather it used a more 'intelligent' method of deciding where to place an end of line than just by chopping any space occurring after column sixty. It would also be useful if we could specify the number of lines per page that we wanted to print and also the number of characters per page and the physical page length. There could be many more features but for the time being we will content ourselves with those listed above.

With the exception of the first modification, all of the features mentioned above are quite easy to implement. To make our printer driver more 'careful' in how it truncates lines we must approach the problem in a totally different way.

Using a character by character approach as we did in program 19 is not going to work. We simply do not have sufficient information using this method. What we will do is to read in the data into an array which will store the data on a word by word basis. In our example a word is defined as being a stream of bytes starting in with a non space character and ending with a space character.

Once this word has been read into the array its length is compared with the space left on the line being printed and if the word fits then it is printed, if there is insufficient space then a new line is output and the word printed at the start of the new line.

This method should give us a much more sensitive printer driver and one which will have a general use.

Program 21 contains the listing for our modified printer driver.

/* program 21 an improved printer driver */

```c
#include stdio/csh;
#define hard "*pr"
int err,d,i,ch,l,pm,lop,noc,page len;
int word[50];
FILE *fp, *ff;

main()
{
  page_len = 66;
  lop = 60;
  noc = 70;
  i=1;
  l = noc;
  err= 0x0d;
  d = 0;
  ch = pm = 1;
  fp = fopen("chpt1c/pcl:1","r");
  ff = fopen(hard,"w");
while( (ch != EOF) )
    {
      ch = getc(fp);
      word[d] = ch;
      putchar(ch);
      ++d;
      if( ch == 0x20 )
          {
            if(d<(l+1))
              {
                print();
              }
            else
              {
                putc(0x0d,ff);
                l=noc;
                ++pm;
                if(pm > lop)new_pge();
                print();
              }
            d=0;
          }
    }
}


    print()
    {
    for(i=0;i<d;++i)
        {
            if(word[i] == 0x0d)
```

```
              {
                putc(word[i],ff);
                l = noc;
                ++pm;
                if(pm > lop)new_pge();
              }
                 else
                    {
                      putc(word[i],ff);
                      --l;
                    }
              }
}


new_page()
{

    for(n=0;n<((page_len+1)-pm);++n)
      {
          putc(0x0d,ff);
      }
    pm = 1;
}
```

The new program starts with the same layout as program 20. There are more variables and an integer array but apart from that they are the same. The array word[50] will be used to contain our incoming data. Otherwise the two files that will be used are exactly the same as in program 20.

There are three functions in the program. These are main(), print() and new page(). As before all the variables are global and so can be accessed from any of the functions.

Function main() begins by setting all the variables to their initial values. The purpose of each of the variables is explained below.

Variable name	Purpose in program
lop	number of lines printed per page.
noc	number of characters printed per line.
l	line space counter.
pm	page counter.
d	word length.
page_len	page length in lines.

i	position in array.
ch	character.

After the variables have been initialised the two file pointers are set. As in program 20 these file pointers are *fp (the pointer to the disk file) and *ff (the pointer to the printer). We have used a predefined file name in this program. In later file handling programs we will look at ways of inputting the file name in an interactive fashion.

The main part of the program consists of a while.......loop. This is used to accept the characters into the array until the end-of-file marker is encountered.

The next statement gets the character from the file (pointed to by fp) and places it into variable ch. It is then placed into the corresponding part of the array and then printed onto the screen by the use of the putchar(ch) statement. The subscript for the array (d) is then increased in value by the use of the prefix increment operator.

All of the program section following this is dependent on whether the character just read was a space or not. This is done by means of the if(ch == 0x20) test. Remember the 0x20 tells the compiler that the character is a hexadecimal 20, which corresponds to a space. In other words the test condition says 'if the last character was a space then do the following'. If the last character was not a space then the while......loop continues and the next character is read in.

Should the last character read be a space then the program section inside the if.....command is carried out. This tests to see if the word will fit into the remaining line by if(d<(l+1)). The reason that l+1 is used is that variable d was incremented after the last character was read and will actually be 1 higher than the true length of the word. Variable l contains the value of the character positions left on the line.

If this test is found to be true (i.e. the word will fit) then the function print() is carried out. Otherwise (the word is too long) and the code following the else... is executed.

This outputs a new line character to the printer by printing a 0x0d (hexadecimal 0d). The putc(err,ff) command is used for this. Once this is done the character position counter is reset and the page counter is incremented. Another test then determines whether the 'end of page' condition has been met. If it has, then control transferred to function new page(). Whether this has to be done or not, control passes to the next statement and function print() is carried out.

After this the variable d is set to zero (for the start of a new word) and the while.....loop continues until the EOF condition is met.

This is the main part of the program, all that remains is for us to look at the way in which each of the two remaining functions operate.

Function print() is the longer of the two and its purpose is to output to the printer the word that has just been read from the file.

It does this by means of a for...loop . The statement for(i=0;i<d;++i) means that the code following this will be carried out while variable i is less than variable d. The reason that the "less than" operator is used is that variable d contains one more than the true word length.

One special condition has to be tested for. This is that the character being printed is actually a new line character or 0x0d. If this is the case then the code following the if(word[i]== 0x0d) test is carried out.

These pieces of code print the character to the printer and then reset the variable l. The page counter is incremented and the test for an 'end of page' is carried out. If this is true then the function new page() is executed.

Should the test for a newline character prove false then the code following the else part of the test is carried out. This outputs the character pointed to by word[i] and then decreases the value of l by one (for each character output). After this, control passes back to the for... loop and the process continues until the whole word has been printed.

Function new_page() is rather more complex than it need be. It was written for a Centronics printer which did not recognise the form feed character. Because of this it was neccessary for a calculation to be carried out, to determine the number of blank lines to output.

The calculation is carried out in the main part of the for.... loop. The test in this loop is n<((pagelen+1)-pm). This gives the number of blank lines. The reason that pagelen+1 is used is that this will generate the one extra line feed that is required to take the printer onto the top of the next page. If this was not used then the pages would 'creep' upwards and produce a very untidy output.

```
/* program 21 CP/M an improved printer driver */

#define EOF -1
#define hard "LST:"
int err,err1,c,d,i,ch,l,pm,lop,noc,page_len;
int word[50];
int *fp, *ff;

main()
{
  page_len = 66;
  lop = 60;
  noc = 70;
  i=1;
  l = noc;
  err= 0x0d;
  err1 = 0x0a;
  d = 0;
```

```
  ch = pm = 1;
  fp = fopen("b:chpt1c.pcl","r");
  ff = fopen(hard,"w");
while( (ch != EOF) )
    {
       ch = getc(fp);
       word[d] = ch;
       putchar(ch);
       ++d;
       if( ch == 0x20 )
          {
             if(d<(l+1))
                {
                     print();
                }
                else
                {
                   putc(err,ff);
                   putc(err1,ff);
                   margin();
                   l=noc;
                   ++pm;
                   if(pm > lop)new_pge();
                   print();
                }
             d=0;
          }
    }
}

    print()
    {
    for(i=0;i<d;++i)
       {
          if((pm==1) && (l==70))margin();
          if(word[i] == 0x0d)
             {
                putc(word[i],ff);
                margin();
                l = noc;
                ++pm;
                if(pm > lop)new_pge();
             }
                else
                {
                   putc(word[i],ff);
                   --l;
                }
          }
```

```
}

new_page()
{
      putc(0x0c,ff);
      putc(err,ff);
      printf("Printer pause type ANY KEY when ready \n");
      c = ci();
      pm = 1;

}

margin()
{
    for(c=1;c<16;c++)
      putc(0x20,ff);
}
```

The CP/M listing of program 21 contains all of the modifications required for program 20 together with some additional features. A new function has been added, which prints a left margin of 15 spaces. The reason for this is that the printer used to test this CP/M driver has a single sheet feeder which loads the paper in with a 10 character offset. If there was no left margin then the leftmost characters on the line would be omitted.

This function is called each time that a new line is generated. The only exception to this is that the function must be called at the start of a document. To determine if the driver is printing the first line of a page, the following test is carried out:-

        if((pm == 1) && (l == 70)margin();

Here the test is whether pm is equal to one (the first line) and whether the line counter is equal to seventy (at the left of the page). If the second part of the test was carried out then function margin() would be executed at the end of each word on line 1.

Function margin() works by printing 15 ASCII 32's out to the printer.

Function new_page() has been modified because the printer used with the CP/M system accepted form feed characters (0x0c). This generates a form feed and after this we print a carriage return character to ensure that the print head is at the lefthand side of the page. The two statements following this are to allow the user to change the paper if this is required. The program simply displays a message onto the screen and then waits for the user to press a key when ready.

The printer driver outlined in program 21 could be improved in a number of ways. The main problem is that the program will crash if a 'word' longer than 50 characters is read in from the disk file. This would occur if, for instance an underline occurred across a whole page or if any other 'document enhancement' produced a full A4 page width.

91

Apart from this problem any number of enhancements could be added. Screen menus, variable page parameters, etc, etc. Since the main purpose of the chapter was to introduce accessing the printer these must be considered suitable 'exercises' for the now (hopefully) confident C programmer.

Apart from the language instruction this chapter illustrates the way in which a few 'simple' improvements to a working program (program 20) can lead to major rethinking and program design (program 21). If all the above modifications were to be included, the final source code could be twice or even three times the length of program 21. Whether the tremendous increase in programming time is warranted is dependent on the application and the needs of the programmer.

Summary of chapter 6.

(1)   The use of additional file pointers to redirect output to the printer.

(2)   The concept of a simple printer driver and a program that achieves this.

(3)   Improvements and modifications to the simple printer driver. An improved printer driver program.

Chapter 7

Direct Access files (almost).

In our chapter on files and filing systems, we looked at sequential files. Strictly speaking these were byte stream files, that is files consisting of a contiguous (continuous and without gaps) stream of bytes of data. Any file of this description has no true records and only becomes a sequential file when some order is imposed on it by the program.

While the byte-stream method has a number of distinct advantages it is very time consuming to have continually to read through the whole file until the particular data that we want appears. The programmer who wishes to implement a rather more sophisticated filing system using C has two options open. The first is to write a direct access filing system in C and the second is to tie in the C program with the operating system of the host machine. In many cases it may only be possible to use the first of these approaches. We will examine the first method in this chapter and the second one in chapter eight.

Our filing system will consist of a program which allows the sequential writing of fixed length records and the direct access of them. This represents a compromise between a fully functioning direct access filing system and one which illustrates some important techniques and allows the programmer much room for modification.

The program code is contained in program 22.

```
/* Program 22 direct access files */

#include stdio/csh;
#option inlib
FILE *fp;
char data[257],*mode,name[15],numb[4],length[4];
int c,d,n,e,i,lrl,rn,k1,k2,k3;


main()
{
    mode = sbrk(2);
    c=1;
    while(c!=EOF && c!= 'e')
    {
      clear();
```

```
            printf("Type <A> to add data to the file \n");
            printf("Type <R> to read the file \n");
            printf("Type <E> to exit \n");
            c = getchar();
                  if( c== 'a') add();
                        else
                              if(c== 'r') read();
                                    else
                                          continue;


      }
}

file_name()
{
      clear();
      printf("PLEASE ENTER THE NAME OF YOUR FILE \n");
      fgets(&name[0],15,stdin);
      clear();
      printf("now enter which mode you wish to use \n");
      printf("<R> to read <A> to append <W> to write \n");
      d=getchar();
      if( d!='r' && d!='a' && d!='w')file name();
      *mode = d;
      ++mode;
      *mode = 0x00;
      --mode;


}


add()
{
      file_name();
      fp = fopen(&name[0],mode);
      clear();
      printf("what record length will you use \n");
      fgets(&length[0],4,stdin);
      lrl=atoi(&length[0]);
      k1=1;
      while(k1!='e')
          {
              fill(&data [0], 257,32);
              clear();
              printf("Please enter your data here \n");
              fgets(&data[0],(lrl+1),stdin);
              for(e=0;e<lrl;++e)
                        {
                              putc(data[e],fp);
```

```
                        }
                printf(" \n \n \nType <E> to end any other key to continue \n");
                k1=getchar();
                if(k1==EOF)break;
        }
fclose(fp);
}
read()

{
        file_name();
        clear();
        printf("what record length will you use \n");
        fgets(&length[0],4,stdin);
        lrl=atoi(&length[0]);
        k2=1;
        while(k2!='e')
           {
             fp= fopen(&name[0],mode);
             fill(&data[0],257,32);
             clear();
             printf("what record number do you want \n");
             fgets(&numb[0],4,stdin);
             rn=atoi(&numb[0]);
             k3=1;
             for(n=0;n<rn;++n)
                 {
                     for(i=0;i<lrl;++i)
                         {
                             if((data[i]=getc(fp))==EOF)
                                 {
                                     fill(&data[0],257,32);
                                     k3=99;
                                     printf("Attempted read past EOF \n");
                                     break;
                                 }
                         }
                     if(k3==99)break;
                 }
             for(n=0;n<lrl;++n)
                 {
                     putchar(data[n]);
                 }
             printf(" \n \n \nType <E> to end any other key to continue \n");
             k2=getchar();
             if(k2==EOF)
                 {
                     fclose(fp);
                     break:
```

```
            }
         fclose(fp);
      }
}

clear()
{
    fill(15360,1023,32);
    cursor(0,0);
```

This program contains much that is familiar and a few new commands and techniques. It consists of five functions and uses the #option inlib for the screen clear routine. Apart from that there are four character arrays, one file pointer, one character pointer and ten integer variables.

The first function is main() and this is really a menu display function. The first statement in it is completely new. This is the mode = sbrk(2); command. The general syntax for this command is:-

    pnt = sbrk(x);

where pnt is a pointer and x is an integer. The command allocates a block of memory of size x bytes. In our example we have allocated a very short block of two bytes to hold the mode of the file that we will be using. The name of the pointer is also mode, to make the program more readable. In our previous filing programs we have always stated the mode of file access as a literal (a character in quotes) ie "r" or "a". To understand why we are going to use the sbrk() command we must look at how C stores the literal in memory.

Any string will be stored in memory as a series of hexadecimal bytes. These will be terminated by a hexadecimal 00. The following will serve as an example.

string	storage in memory
"Hello"	48 65 6C 6C 6F 00
"Goodbye"	47 6F 6F 64 62 79 65 00

What we want to be able to do is to accept the mode that the user wants, from the keyboard and use this in a flexible fopen() command. We could try using the fgets() function but this has a major drawback, it places a hexadecimal 0D at the end of the string. This will not be accepted in the fopen() command.

The technique that we will use will be to load one character into the memory space set aside by sbrk() and then load a hexadecimal 00 into the following memory location. This will have the same effect as if we had declared the mode as a literal string. We can the load this value into our fopen() function by using the address pointed to by our pointer *mode. (it will of course be necessary for us to decrement the value of the pointer by one, since it would otherwise point to the 00 character).

The second statement sets variable c to 1 and then the while..... part of the main control loop is begun. this sets two exit conditions for this loop. The loop will be terminated if c is equal to either EOF or 'e'.

The first statement of the loop clears the screen and then three printf() commands display the various options onto the screen.

The user's response is picked up by the c = getchar() command. A series of if.... statements then filter the response and carry out the relevant function call if the test evaluates to true. Should the user press some other key then the program continues and the loop reiterates, the process continuing until an acceptable key response is made.

There are two possible function calls that can be executed. These are add() and read(). The other function file_name() is called by both add() and read().

Function add() is the one that will add records to the file. It begins with a call to function file_name() which prompts the user to enter the file name and the mode of access. The file name is returned in character array name[], and the mode is returned via the pointer *mode. This enables the second statement to open the file in the mode requested. As in our previous filing examples if the file is opened in mode "w" any existing data will be overwritten by the writing process.

The screen is then cleared and the user prompted to enter the record length of the file. This is entered into array length[] and is then converted into an integer by the use of the atoi() function. After this function integer variable lrl contains the record length of the file.

The next section of the program is essentially a while.... loop that allows the user to continually add records until they reply 'e' to the "continue?" prompt. Variable k1 is set equal to 1 at the start of the while.... loop, and the main body of the loop is executed.

This starts by setting all of array data[] equal to blanks (ASCII 32's) this allows any unused array space to be written to the disk in a 'tidy' format. Remember, since we are going to emulate a direct access file we will have to use fixed length records and any unused record space will still be written to disk.

The user is then prompted to enter the data and this is loaded into the array data[] by using the fgets() function. Once this has been entered it is written to disk by means of a putc() function inside a for.... loop. This gives us more control over the data written to disk and allows the data to be written in a 'byte stream' fashion, in blocks equal to the logical record length.

After this disk write routine the user is prompted with a message instructing them to type <E> to end data entry or any other key to continue. Pressing either <E> or <BRK> will terminate the function and close the file.

The reason that the fgets() function uses lrl+1 as a data entry parameter is that the fgets() function enters 1 less than the value specified. This would cause a short logical record length in those situations where the full amount of data was going to be entered.

The second file handling function is read() and this is the more complex of the two. We stated earlier that the file handling program was sequential in the way that it handled writing data to disk but it directly accessed that data. It is because of this that function read() is more complex.

The function starts in the same way as function add() that is with a call to function file_name(). This returns the file name and mode as before. Following this the screen is cleared and the user is asked what record length is being used. The need to ask for the record length is due to the fact that this data is not stored on the disk as a permanent marker. The computer still treats the data on disk as a byte stream file, it is we who are trying to impose some additional 'structure' on it.

As before, the record length is loaded into array length[] and then converted into integer variable lrl. The majority of the read() function consists of a series of loops. The first is a while...... loop and variable k2 is the data item used to test for the exit condition. K2 is initialised and then the loop begins.

The file pointer fp is initialised by the fopen() command which opens the file each time the loop is executed. The file is opened in the mode specified by file_name(). It should be pointed out that no error trapping has been done here, thus it is possible to open the file in mode "w" or "a" and then an attempt made to read the file. The exact result of this type of operation is dependent on the compiler but normally some type of havoc will result, possibly causing destruction of the file.

Function fill () loads array data[] with ASCII blanks to clear the data area. This is simply to make the data appear more 'presentable' to us and also to avoid the type of situation where a previous data read loaded in, say, the full amount of characters and a successive read only loaded a few. The previous read would still leave some 'residual' characters in the array. After that the screen is cleared and the user is asked what record number is required. This is entered into array numb[] and converted into integer rn by using the atoi function. Variable k3 is then set to 1, to prevent it 'carrying over' any residual value into one of the test loops.

The second of the loops is now entered. This is a for.... loop and it serves to count through the data stream until the correct record has been reached. The diagram below will help to illustrate this point.

43 65 67 36 18 6F 6D 6E 76 54 25 5E 1F 56 34 27 18 28 46

An imaginary byte stream file is pictured above. Let us suppose that the file was divided into five byte records. To access the third record the first two records would have to be read through.

These two records would contain 2 X 5 or 10 bytes. By the same reasoning, to access the 30th record we would have to read through 29 X 5 or 145 bytes. The equation for determining the number of bytes to read is:-

number of bytes = (rec-1) X LRL

where rec is the record number desired and LRL is the logical record length of the file.

In our loop we will read in the lrl of data bytes rn times. The loop will then end with array data[ ]containing the last block of bytes i.e. the one we wanted. The outer for.... loop counts the record number and the inner loop loads in the correct number of bytes from the lrl. Variable n is used for the outer loop and variable i for the inner one.

One test condition is carried out. This tests for the end of the file. If this occurs, then the array is cleared, a warning message is printed and the inner loop is exited by means of the break; command. Variable k3 is also set to 99 (an arbitrary value). This is tested for in the outer loop and if it is found to be true then the outer loop is also exited.

In this way the program simply reads through the data file until the required block of data is found. When this happens the loops are exited and the next loop entered. The purpose of this loop is to print out the contents of the array onto the screen by means of the putchar() function.

Once this is done the user is presented with the choice of continuing or terminating, and the response is entered into variable k2. If this is equal to either <E> or <BRK> then the file is closed and the function is terminated.

The last function that we will look at is function file name(). This is the function that accepts both the name of the file and the logical record length from the user.

This function starts by clearing the screen and prompting the user to enter the name of the file. Function fgets () is used to enter the response into array name[ ]. Up to 14 chatacters may be entered. This is sufficient for standard file names like:-

      b:test.dat
      sample/dat:3

etc. Since only eight characters may be entered for the main file name this allows the full range of possibilities. Once the name has been entered the screen is cleared and the user is prompted for the mode of the file. Only one of three characters is allowed. "A" for append, "W" for write and "R" for read. The user's response is entered into variable d and this is tested to see if it is one of the correct entries. If it is not, then the function is called again and will continue to be called until a correct entry is made.

Once a correct response has been made the data item stored in d is loaded into the memory location pointed to by mode. This pointer is then incremented and the next memory location is loaded with a hexadecimal 00. The pointer is then decremented so that any reference to mode will return the character entered by the user.

After this the function ends and control passes back to the calling function with the file name stored in array name[] and the file mode pointed to by the pointer 'mode'.

```
/* Program 22 CP/M direct access files */

#define stdout 1
#define stdin 0
#define EOF -1
#define CTRL 3
int fp;
char data[257],*mode,name[15];
int ck,c,d,n,e,i,lrl,rn,k1,k2,k3;


main()
{
    mode = malloc(2);
    c=1;
    while(c!=CTRL && c!= 'e')
    {
    clear();
    printf("Type <A> to add data to the file \n");
    printf("Type <R> to read the file \n");
    printf("Type <E> to exit \n");
    c = ci();
        if( c== 'a') add();
            else
                if(c== 'r') readn();
                    else
                        continue;

    }
}

file_name()
{
    clear();
    printf("PLEASE ENTER THE NAME OF YOUR FILE \n");
    fgets(&name[0],15,stdin);
    clear();
    printf("now enter which mode you wish to use \n");
    printf("<R>to read <A> to append <W> to write \n");
    d=ci();
    if( d!='r' && d!='a' && d!='w')file name();
```

```c
        *mode = d;
        ++mode;
        *mode = 0x00;
        --mode;

}


add()
{
        file_name();
        fp = fopen(&name[0],mode);
        clear();
        printf("what record length will you use \n");
        scanf("%d4",&lrl);
        k1=1;
        while(k1!='e')
            {
                _setmem(&data[0],257,00);
                clear();
                printf("Please enter your data here \n");
                fgets(&data[0],(lrl+1),stdin);
                sl = strlen(&data[0]);
                data[sl] = 0x0a;
                for(e=0;e<rl;++e)
                        {
                                putc(data[e],fp);
                        }
                printf("\n \n \nType <E> to end any other key to continue \n");
                k1=ci();
                if(k1==CTRL)break;
            }
fclose(fp);
}


readn()

{

        file_name();
        clear();
        printf("what record length will you use \n");
        scanf("%d4",&lrl);
        k2=1;
        while(k2!='e')
            {
                fp= fopen(&name[0],mode);
                _setmem(&data[0],257,00);
```

```
                clear();
                printf("what record number do you want \n");
                scanf("%d4",&rn);
                k3=1;
                for(n=0;n<rn;++n)
                    {
                        for(i=0;i<lrl;++i)
                            {
                                if((ck =getc(fp))==EOF)
                                {
                                    _setmem(&data[0],257,00);
                                    k3=99;
                                    printf("Attempted read past EOF \ n");
                                    break;
                                }
                            else
                                data[i] = ck;
                        }
                        if(k3==99)break;
                    }
                for(n=0;n<lrl;++n)
                    {
                        putchar(data[n]);
                    }
                printf(" \n \n \nType <E> to end any other key to continue \n");
                k2=ci();
                if(k2==CTRL)
                        {
                            fclose(fp);
                            break;
                        }
                fclose(fp);
            }
        }


clear()
{
    scr_clr();
    scr_rowcol(0,0);
}
```

Once again the CP/M version of our 'direct access' filing system is almost identical to the LC version. One or two points do, however, need clarification.

The method used to allocate memory space is a little different. The DeSmet compiler uses a function called malloc instead of the sbrk function. Apart from the different titles they act in exactly the same way (that of allocating a block of memory).

The read() function has been changed to avoid a clash with a standard DeSmet function. The new function name is readn().

Function file name() is the same in both versions apart from the correction for the fgets() function discussed in an earlier chapter. This simply adds the LF (line feed) character to the data input to array name.

A number of differences occur in function add(). These are the use of the scanf() function to accept the logical record length of the file. This replaces the two statements (fgets() and atoi()) in the LC program version. The format of "%d4" tells the compiler to accept a four digit integer into the data item pointed to. The overall effect of this is the same as in the previous program. The setmem() function is used to clear the data array, and the fgets() function is modified as before.

Function readn() makes use of the scanf() command and contains all of the modifications and adjustments mentioned previously. One important change is that the test if((data[i]=getc(fp))==EOF) will not work. The reason for this is that the EOF test will return a value of -1 (a signed integer). The LC compiler was quite happy to accept this into a character variable and test accordingly. The DeSmet compiler does not like returning the -1 into a character variable. The way round this is illustrated in the program. The value returned is placed in an integer variable and if this is not the EOF value then the data stored in the integer is placed into the corresponding element of the character array. Storing an integer into a character simply 'chops off' the most significant byte. This is perfectly acceptable since our data is all stored in the least significant byte of the integer.

This relatively short program has introduced you to the basic ideas behind constructing a direct access filing system in C. Some dedicated filing languages (notably COBOL) allow the programmer to construct files which can be either direct access or sequential access or both, depending on the programmer's requirements. Our program 22 has perhaps given some indication as to how this seemingly impossible task can be developed.

There are some glaring omissions, notably in the error trapping but it was thought that the inclusion of these routines would only confuse the essential point of the chapter, that of constructing a direct access file.

With a little additional programming many additional 'enhancements' could be added to the program. These are left to the reader to experiment with by way of an exercise.

Summary of chapter 7.

(1)   The introduction of the sbrk() function and its use.

(2)   The structure of byte stream files and how they can be interpreted as fixed length records.

(3)   Adding data to the file by means of a previously defined fixed length data block.

(4)   The method of determining the position of a particular record within the file. The use of the logical record length and the record number to access the required record.

(5)   Literal storage and a method of direct data entry to a defined memory location.

Chapter 8

Direct Access Files.

In the previous chapter we looked at a method for producing what appeared to be direct access files. This used a method of "byte offset" calculation to determine the position of each record in the file.

The present chapter will develop a filing system based around the direct access file control commands provided by the operating system. The commands used are those in the LDOS operating system. They will not be the same for computers using other operating systems but the principles behind the techniques will remain the same.

How LDOS controls files.

The 'standard' micro computer systems allow physical record lengths from 1 to 256 bytes. LDOS will also allow the logical records in a direct access file to 'span' the physical records. This provides for much more efficient usage of disk space while maintaining the benefits of direct access records. The principle can be seen in the diagram below:-

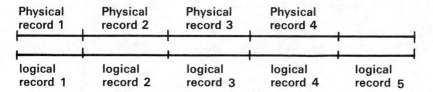

Physical record 1	Physical record 2	Physical record 3	Physical record 4	
logical record 1	logical record 2	logical record 3	logical record 4	logical record 5

We have seen that byte input/output can be carried out on disk files, to the printer, to the screen and from the keyboard. In fact the C language allows us to use byte i/o to any device, where a device is any mechanical, electrical or logical structure that is handling data.

Whenever we have used files in the previous programs we have done two things. (1) declared a file pointer by the command FILE *fp or FILE *ff. (Any suitable variable name could be used instead of fp or ff in the examples). (2) used a file name when accessing any disk files.

The reasons for these two actions are that the disk operating system requires a file specification or 'filespec' to enable it to access the disk control system. In LDOS this filespec has four components.

(1) A primary file name which may contain up to eight characters. The only restriction is that the first character must be an alphabetic character, the remainder can be either alphabetic or numeric.

(2) An optional extension may be included. This is separated from the primary filename by the slash '/' character. Typically this is used to designate file types eg /ccc for C source files /asm for assembler files and so on.

(3) An optional eight character password. This is separated from the options above by a period '.'. In our examples this feature will not be catered for.

(4) An optional 2 character drive extension. The first character here must be a colon. The second character must be a number specifying the drive required.

The following are legal LDOS file names.

```
SAMPLE/DAT.KEVS:2
SCREEN/ASM:4
DATE/CCC:1
```

Whenever the programmer accesses a disk file the file specification is loaded into a 32-byte buffer called the file control block (FCB). In other operating systems, and in general use, this type of structure is called a device control block (DCB).

The command FILE *fp sets aside a 32 byte buffer that is pointed to by the pointer *fp. All that a buffer is, is a block of memory that will be used for a specific purpose, normally the temporary storage of data.

Whenever a file is opened the FCB is loaded with the filespec which is then loaded into one of the Z80 processor's registers. The register used is DE which must point to the first byte of the FCB before the file is opened. (if you are unsure what a register is consult a book on machine code programming with the Z80 chip. Basically, a register is a one or two byte piece of memory in the chip that is used to pass parameters in machine code programs).

Once the register has been loaded with the address of the first byte of the FCB a machine code routine is called which will open the file. The processor looks for a terminator in the FCB. This has to be either a hexadecimal 03 or a hexadecimal 0D. If either of these are missing then the file will not be opened.

The other registers that our programs will use are the BC and HL registers. These will be used to hold information such as the logical record length, record number and various buffer parameters.

There are a number of machine code routines used in this program. They are all standard operating system commands and will be declared at the start of the program. The definitions will be presented in as meaningful a way as possible. eg:-

#define OPEN 0X4424   This is the open file routine which starts at memory location 4424 (hex).

#define READ 0X4436   This is the read-file routine which starts at memory location 4436 (hex).

All of the usage of the other registers will be explained as we examine each part of program 23.

```
/* Program 23 a real direct access system */
/* Based on a system supplied by Eric Meyer */
#include stdio/csh
#option inlib
#define FSPEC 0X441C
#define OPEN 0X4424
#define INIT 0X4420
#define CLOSE 0X4428
#define WRITE 0X4439
#define POSN 0X4442
#define READ 0X4436
#define AF 0
#define BC 1
#define DE 2
#define HL 3
#define IX  4
#define IY  5

char *fp;
int rc,rn,lrl,c,n,*regs[6];
char *recptr,*buf,*fspec,*lrc,*rec;

main()
{
   recptr=sbrk(257);
   fspec=sbrk(18);
   lrc=sbrk(5);
   fp=sbrk(32);
   rec=sbrk(5);
   buf=sbrk(257);
   clear();
   get name();
   regs[HL] = fspec;
   regs[DE] = fp;
   if(( rc = call(FSPEC,regs))!=0)
        printf("error rc = %d \n",rc);
```

```
                else
                  {
                    regs[HL] = buf;
                    regs[DE] = fp;
                    regs[BC] = lrl<<8;
                    call(INIT,regs);
                    get data();
                    dclose();
                  }
    }


dclose()
{
    regs[DE]=fp;
    call(CLOSE,regs);
    clear();
    printf("Job Done !!! \n");
}


get_name()
{
    printf("FILE name CCCCCCCC/EEE:D \n");
    printf("                ");
    fgets(fspec,15,stdin);
    printf(" now the Logical record length \n");
    fgets(lrc,4,stdin);
    lrl=atoi(lrc);
}


get_data()
{
    n=99;
    while(n!='n')
      {
clear();
    printf("now the record number please \n");
        fgets(rec,4,stdin);
        rn=atoi(rec);
        --rn;
        regs[DE]=fp;
        regs[BC]=rn;
        call(POSN,regs);
        printf("now enter the data please/n");
        fill(recptr,257,32);
        fgets(recptr,(lrl+1),stdin);
        regs[HL]=recptr;
```

```
        call(WRITE,regs);
        printf("enter more data <n> to end \n");
        n=getchar();
        if(n==EOF)break;

    }
}


clear()
{
    fill(15360,1023,32);
    cursor(0,0);
}
```

This program is designed to create a direct access filing system which can have user-specified logical record length and file name. All of the various operating system calls have been included for the sake of completeness although not all of them will be used.

The first part of the program contains all of the #include, #option and #define statements. The #define statements are all #self explanatory with the exception of the POSN definition. This is the machine language call that will be used to position the file at the required record number. It is necessary to do this before a file record can be read or written.

The last six #define statements may seem a little odd. In fact they are designed to help the programmer by allowing explicit reference to the various registers of the processor. The way that these registers are accessed is to use a call() function, supplied as part of the #option inlib library. The exact syntax for this command is as follows.

        retcode = call(address,regs);

Where retcode is the value returned by the function, address is the address of the machine language program called by our function and regs is an integer array of dimension six (the alternative is to use a character array of dimension twelve). The data value to be passed to each of the register pairs is held in array regs. The data to be passed to registers AF would be held in regs[0], that for registers BC in regs[1] and so on. The numbers shown in the #define statements correspond directly to the relative position in array regs.

The remainder of our first program section declares all of the variables and pointers that we are going to use. There are a large number of pointers since we are going to be doing a lot of work with memory positions, and pointers provide the easiest method of dealing with this.

The program consists of five functions, including the short clear screen function which will not be explained. Function main() begins by declaring the various blocks of memory used by the program. These represent, in order, the buffer for data transfer to and from disk, the filespec buffer, the logical record length store, the file control block, the record number store, and a second buffer to hold file transfer data.

The variables on the left of these sbrk() commands are the pointers to each of the memory blocks. Following the set up of the respective memory blocks the screen is cleared and the function get_name() is carried out. This returns with the file name in buffer fspec and the logical record number held in variable lrl. In comparing this file program with some of the others it would appear that we have left out the FILE pointer command that has been used in all of our previous programs. This is a deliberate omission. It was stated at the start of the chapter that the operating system expects to find a buffer of 32 bytes to hold the filespec. Normally this is set up by using the FILE *fp, or comparable, command. All that we have done is to assign our own 32 byte buffer referenced by the pointer fp. This will be used to hold the file spec. This simply shows that there is very little in the C language that cannot be rewritten or restructured if we so desire. Once the basic principles of a problem have been understood the programmer is given an almost unlimited range of flexibility in the possible solutions.

After the function get_name() has been executed the array regs is set to the relevant values. At the moment we are only interested in using the HL and DE registers. The values held by pointers fspec and fp are loaded into regs[HL] and regs[DE] by the two statements:-

```
regs[HL] = fspec;
regs[DE] = fp;
```

When the FSPEC routine is called the data in fspec will be transferred to the FCB and the correct FCB terminator will be added. Should something be wrong with our file spec then the retcode of the call statement will return a value other than zero.

The statement following the regs initialisation calls up the routine that we want and transfers the data held by regs[]. The statement

```
if(( rc = call(FSPEC,regs))!=0)
```

carries out the call to the address specified by the #defined value of FSPEC and returns the value into variable rc. As we said earlier, if this is not successful, for whatever reason, rc will contain a value other than zero. If this happens then the warning message will be printed and the program terminated.

If the filespec is transferred to the FCB correctly then the block of commands following the else part of the test are carried out. These consist of another set of register initialisations and need to be explained in detail.

The set up of the registers ready for the next call are as follows:-

ARRAY	REGISTER AFFECTED	PURPOSE
regs[HL]	HL	Points to the files 'standard' i/o buffer.
regs[DE]	DE	Points to the FCB.
regs[BC]	BC	The logical record length is stored in register B.

The registers are initialised with the values held in each of the respective pointers. When the machine language routine INIT is called the file pointed to by register DE is opened if it exists. If it is not present on the disk then it will be created by the routine. There is a separate open routine that will not create the file if it does not exist. This will only be used when we attempt to read the file.

There is one additional feature of the last register assignation that needs explanation. This is the <<8 command. C has a number of commands that are called 'bitwise' operators, this means that they deal with the individual bits of a byte or bytes. We will only deal with the operator defined above since these operators are outside the scope of this book. The reason for using this operator is that the registers referred to above are in fact double registers or more correctly register pairs. The pair BC consist of an eight bit register B and an eight bit register C. If we used the assignation regs[BC] = 34, then the value 34 would be stored into register C. Our disk operating system expects the value of the logical record length to be placed into the B register. This means that we have to move the value from register C into register B. The operator <<8 will shift the binary data in the register pair eight places to the left. This is illustrated below.

REGISTER PAIR

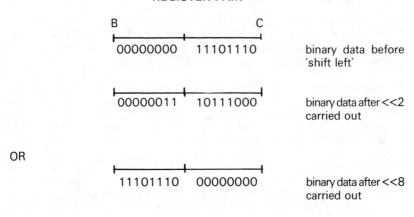

From this diagram it should be clear that whatever integer value follows the <<
(left shift operator) represents the number of digit positions to be shifted. After the
application of the <<8 operator register B will contain the logical record length.
This is exactly what we wanted and will allow the correct record length to be
created on disk.

Following these register assignments a machine language call is made that calls
the routine INIT and either creates and opens the file, or simply opens it if it already
exists.

The next statement transfers program control to function get data(). Once this
function has finished, the file is closed and the program terminates. All that this
program does is to create a file and write data to it. By using the list command in
LDOS (preferably specifying the HEX option) the file can be examined.

The second function in our program is dclose() and this closes the file and
terminates the program. The only register used by this function is regs[DE] which
is set equal to the file pointer, fp. Once this has been done then the call is made to
routine CLOSE. This closes the file after which the screen is cleared and a 'Job
Done' message printed onto the screen.

The get_name() function is very similar to the corresponding function in our
previous filing program. It enables the user to enter the name and drive
specification of the file into the program. In addition to this, it asks for the logical
record length of the file.

The function starts by displaying a 'FILE name' prompt onto the screen. This is
followed (in the same printf statement) by a description of the file name format.
The next statement prints a blank line onto the screen without a new line
command. This acts as a spacing block so that whatever the user types in appears
under the format descriptor on the screen. The main purpose of this is an attempt
to assist the new user to the type of file format required. It has no direct relevance
to our filing method.

An fgets() function then inputs the data directly into the memory block pointed to
by the fspec pointer. We are only using a 15 character limit on the fgets() since we
are not interested in entering any passwords. By extending the limit of the fgets()
statement passwords could be entered into the file name.

The printf() statement displays a prompt onto the screen to allow the user to
directly enter the logical record length into the program. This is loaded directly into
the memory location specified by the pointer lrc. Once loaded it is converted into
an integer, as before, by an atoi() operation. The variable lrl then contains the
integer value of the logical record length.

The final function in this section is get data() and this is the function that is used to
get the data from the user and write it out to disk. The main part of this function
consists of a while.... loop which prompts the user to continue or end after each
data record has been written out to disk.

The function begins by setting variable n to 99. This is the usual initialisation at the start of a loop. The loop starts with a screen clear and the record number prompt is printed onto the screen. One of the benefits of accessing the operating system's direct access routines is that they enable us to enter and record numbers. If we entered record 67 as our first record number the computer would skip the equivalent of 66 records before writing the 67th. Our simple direct access system in the previous chapter could not have dealt with this and it only allowed a 'sequential' writing of records. Any attempt at making this more sophisticated would have meant a considerable amount of additional programming.

An fgets() and atoi() function are used to accept the user's record number. The atoi() function places the integer value into the variable rn. After this rn is decremented. This may seem strange, but before any writing or reading of the file can be done we must position the disk 'head' in the correct position. By decrementing variable rn by a --rn statement we can now position the disk 'head' to the last record. When the write process begins we will write the next record and all will be in order. This means that the first record in the file will be stored on disk as record number '0'. Our other programs in this chapter will also treat the file structure accordingly.

Once the two registers DE and BC have been loaded with the values of pointers fp and rn, a call to routine POSN then positions the disk 'head' and the data is entered into the buffer.

The data is entered into the buffer pointed to by recptr and a limit of (lrl+1) is used for the same reasons as in chapter 7. The two statements before the fgets() are to display a prompt onto the screen and to clear the buffer of any random characters. As before this is done by means of a fill() command which places a series of ASCII 32's into the memory locations. After the data has been entered the register HL is loaded with the pointer recptr, to point to the start of the buffer and a call to routine WRITE is made. This writes the data to disk. A new prompt is displayed onto the screen allowing the user to enter <N> to terminate the loop. The EOF or <BRK> key is trapped for in the usual way.

Although program 23 allows us to create and write to a direct access disk file it does not allow both reading and writing to and from the file. Program 24 does both, it is a menu driven program and will allow the creation, and general access, of any disk file. Although it is not a fully error trapped or 'user proof' program, it does illustrate the full requirements for a direct access filing system linked into the host operating system.

```
/* Program 24 direct read and write */

#include stdio/csh
#option inlib
#define FSPEC 0X441C
#define OPEN 0X4424
#define INIT 0X4420
```

```c
#define CLOSE 0X4428
#define WRITE 0X4439
#define POSN 0X4442
#define READ 0X4436
#define AF 0
#define BC 1
#define DE 2
#define HL 3
#define IX 4
#define IY 5
char *fp;
int i,rc,rn,lrl,c,n,n2;
char *recptr,*regs[12],*buf,*fspec,*lrc,*rec;

main()
{
    recptr=sbrk(257);
    fspec=sbrk(18);
    lrc=sbrk(5);
    fp=sbrk(32);
    rec=sbrk(5);
    buf=sbrk(256);
    clear();
    c=1;
    while(c!='e' && c!=EOF)
        {
            printf("Type <W> to write to the file \n");
            printf("Type <R> to read from the file \n");
            printf("Type <E> to end \n");
            c=getchar();
            if(c!='w' && c!='r' && c!='e' && c!=EOF)main();
              if(c=='e' || c==EOF)break;
                else
                    {
                        get_name();
                        open();
                    }
        }
}


open()
{
    regs[HL] = fspec;
    regs[DE] = fp;
    if(( rc = call(FSPEC,regs))!=0)
        printf("error rc = %d \n",rc);
            else
                {
```

114

```
                    regs[HL] = buf;
                    regs[DE] = fp;
                    regs[BC] = lrl<<8;
                    if(c=='w')
                        {
                            call(INIT,regs);
                            get_data();
                        }
                        else
                            {
                                call(OPEN,regs);
                                read data();
                            }
dclose();
                }
}


dclose()
{
    regs[DE]=fp;
    call(CLOSE,regs);
    clear();
}


get_name()
{
    clear();
    printf("FILE name CCCCCCCC/EEE:D \n");
    printf("");
    fgets(fspec,15,stdin);
    printf("now the Logical record length \n");
    fgets(lrc,4,stdin);
    lrl=atoi(lrc);
}


get_data()
{
    n=99;
    while(n!='n' && n !=EOF)
    {
        clear();
        rec_numb();
        rec_pos();
        printf("now enter the data please \n");
        fill(recptr,257,32);
        fgets(recptr,(lrl+1),stdin);
```

```
            regs[HL]=recptr;
            call(WRITE,regs);
            printf("enter more data <n> to end \n");
            n=getchar();
        }
}


clear()
{
    fill(15360,1023,32);
    cursor(0,0);
}

read_data()
{
    n2=99;
    while(n2!='n' && n2!=EOF)
{
    rec_numb();
    rec_pos();
    clear();
    fill(recptr,257,32);
    regs[HL]=recptr;
    if(rc=(call(READ,regs))!=C)

        {
            clear();
            printf("ERROR DURING READ !!!!!! \n");
            printf("\n \nPRESS ANY KEY TO CONTINUE\n");
            n2=getchar();
        }
      else
        {
            puts(recptr);
            printf("\n \nenter more data <N> to end. \n");
            n2=getchar();
        }
    }
}


rec_numb()
{
    clear();
    printf("now the record number please \n");
    fgets(rec,4,stdin);
    rn=atoi(rec);
    --rn;
```

```
}
rec_pos()
{
    regs[DE]=fp;
    regs[BC]=rn;
    call(POSN,regs);
}
```

Program 24 is essentially the same as program 23, with a different structure and an additional function added to it. It has been made menu driven to allow the user to select the action wanted. Some essential error trapping has been included and where relevant diagnostic messages are printed out. There are a number of places where additional errors could be coded for, but it was not thought necessary to include these in the program itself.

There are now eight program functions in our direct access read/write program. The first of these is main() and its purpose is to assign pointers to the various memory blocks,display the menu and accept the user's response. The menu display is our usual one and the error trapping in the form of the statement :-

if(c!='w' && c!='r' && c!='e' && c!=EOF)

should be familiar. An additional trap line allows the menu loop to be exited if either the <BRK> or <E> keys are pressed. If the user's response is either 'w' or 'r' then the function getname() is called. This accepts the file name and the logical record length from the user in exactly the same way as in program 23. Once the file name and record length have been entered, function open() is carried out.

Function open() is similar to the sequence of code in function main() of program 23. In it the registers HL and DE are loaded and a call to routine FSPEC is made. After this, registers HL, DE and BC are loaded. A test is made on the value of variable c. If this is equal to 'w' then the user has selected the write option. In this option we want the disk file to be created if it does not exist. To achieve this we use routine INIT, as before. Following this function getdata() is carried out and data is entered into the file in exactly the same way as in program 23. Should the test on variable c prove false (i.e. the key pressed was not 'w') then the else part of the test is carried out. This means that the user must have selected option 'r' and so the file should not be created if it does not exist on disk. This is done by calling routine OPEN and then carrying out function read data() which allows the user to read selected records from disk.

With the exception of function read_data() the remaining functions are identical to the corresponding code sections in program 23 and will not be explained further. Function read data() consists of a while.... loop which repeatedly allows the user to enter a record number. This is done by function rec_numb() which is the same code as the previous program. Once this has been done, function rec_pos() positions the disk 'head' ready for the read. The screen is cleared and the buffer, recptr, filled with ASCII blanks. Register HL is loaded with the buffer's address and a call to routine READ is made. If this is successful (i.e. the return code, stored in variable rc, is equal to zero) the data contained in the buffer is printed onto the screen, by means of a puts(recptr) statement. The user prompt is displayed and pressing any key allows the read loop to continue. If keys <N> or <BRK> are pressed then the routine terminates.

It is necessary to error trap the READ routine because it would otherwise be possible for the user to enter a record number outside the range on the file. By using the error trap expression

if(rc=(call(READ,regs)) !=0)

variable rc will have a value other than zero if this occurs. In circumstances where this does happen, the screen is cleared and the warning message is printed. The user is then prompted to either re-enter the record number or to terminate the loop. Control then passes back to the menu.

This is the end of our basic direct access filing system. Among the other functions that we could have included are machine code routines for sequential disk writing (these write the next record and then automatically update the record pointer), various functions allowing the user to update existing records and routines for allowing complex (more than one) fields per record. These, together with more sophisticated error trapping and more detailed screen messages, could be used to produce a very complex and flexible filing system.

The C language can be made to communicate directly with the environment that it is running in. This is almost always a disk operating system of some sort or other. By allowing the user access to the more useful routines, the language can be made to have all of the features of other languages, e.g. the filing flexibility of COBOL or the mathematical power of FORTRAN or PASCAL. The programmer can pick and chose whichever functions are needed and then 'tailor' these to the particular purpose required.

Summary of Chapter 8.

(1) Direct access files. Why C can't deal with them as standard.

(2) A method for producing a 'pseudo' direct access filing system.

(3) The use of the sbrk() function in assigning memory blocks for use as data buffers.

(4) Linking the C program with an operating system.

(5) File Control Blocks what they are and how to handle them.

(6) The construction of a direct access program to create and write data to a disk file.

(7) A direct access filing program that allows both the reading and writing of direct access records to a disk file.

Chapter 9

Command Line Arguments.

In many programs it would be very useful if we could pass some parameters to the program itself directly from the operating system. For instance, if we had a program called COPY, which copied a file to some other device or file then we could simply type the following command:-

    COPY FILE-1 FILE-2

and the program would proceed to execute and copy the contents of FILE-1 onto FILE-2. In a similar way we could type :-

    COPY FILE-1 PRINTER

where the word PRINTER was used to direct the output of the copying process to the printer.

The above examples serve to illustrate a simple application of the technique whereby a large number of additional commands could be added to the structure of the operating system.

C provides us with a sophisticated method of dealing with this type of situation. It does this by means of two arguments (parameters) that can be passed to the function main() at the start of execution. The two arguments are 'argc' and 'argv', where argc is an integer containing the number of command line arguments and argv is a pointer to an array of characters strings each of which contains the arguments in question.

Since the command line will always have to have at least one statement (the program title), argc will have a value of at least 1. This means that when referencing the array argv we will have to remember that its first element is going to be argv[0] and adjust our parameters accordingly.

The following examples should make the values held by argc and argv clearer.

COMMAND LINE	HELLO THIS IS A TEST
ARGC VAL	5
ARGV[0]	HELLO
ARGV[1]	THIS

ARGV[2]	IS
ARGV[3]	A
ARGV[4]	TEST
COMMAND LINE	COPY THISFILE THATFILE
ARGC	3
ARGV[0]	COPY
ARGV[1]	THISFILE
ARGV[2]	THATFILE

Program 25 further illustrates the concepts behind argc and argv.

```
/* Program 25 command lines */
/* modified from Kernighan & Ritchie the C programming language */
#include stdio/csh
main(argc, argv)
int argc;
char *argv[];
{
      printf("The value of argc is %d \n",argc);
      printf("The command line is \n");
      while(--argc > 0)
            printf("%s%c", *++argv, (argc > 1) ? ' ' : '\n');
}
```

The way in which the values of argc and argv are passed can be seen quite clearly. They are treated as if they were any normal parameters, and declared in the lines following the function name. As we would expect, argc is declared as an integer and argv as an array of pointers.

The first line in the program simply prints out the value of argc. This is a straight-forward usage of the printf statement and needs no further explanation. The statements making up the while...loop do need some clarification since they represent a technique that will be used in most of the remaining program examples. The method of declaring an undimensioned array as [] means that the array is of undetermined length. In this way no upper limit (within the machine's capabilities) is set on the array.

The control part of the while...loop consists of the statement :-
      while(--argc > 0)

This decrements argc and executes the body of the loop as long as argc is greater than zero. Remembering that the largest index of argv is 1 less than argc this means that when argc is equal to zero there will be no more arguments to print.

The next new statement is the *++argv one. By using the '*' prefix we are going to deliver the contents of the address pointed to by ++argv (remember that argv is an array of pointers, each pointing to one of the arguments passed from the command line). The purpose of using ++argv is that we are not interested in using the first argument (the program name). It is because argv is set to the value of the first element in the array at the time that the program begins that we can simply state ++argv to point to the second argument. In other words, the value of argv at execution time will always be the storage location of the program name.

The final part of the loop body is the statement

$$(argc > 1) ? ' ' : '\backslash n'$$

which illustrates one of the more subtle operators explained in chapter 3. It replaces an if...else construction, if argc is greater than 1 then a space is printed and if not, then a new line is printed. The effect is to print out the arguments of the command line with spaces between them and ending in a new line character.

```
/* Program 25 CP/M command lines */
/* modified from Kernighan & Ritchie the C programming language */
main(argc, argv)
int argc;
char *argv[];
{
    printf("The value of argc is %d \n",argc);
    printf("The command line is. \n");
    while(--argc > 0)
        printf("%s%c", *++argv, (argc > 1) ? ' ' : '\n');
}
```

The CP/M version once again illustrates how few modifications are needed to convert from one compiler to another.

The next program example is a modification of the GREP program (available in UNIX). It was converted to LC by Frank Shannon and made available by the LC user's group. What it does is to search a named file for the text specified. Both the text and the file are specified in the command line.

Before we begin, a few words about the input/output redirection of LC.

It is possible to specify a file for input or output by the following syntax on the command line:-

<file1	inputs from file 1
<another	inputs from file 'another'
>test/dat	outputs to file test/dat
>*pr	outputs to the device (printer)

This feature is rather unusual since it means that we do not have to allow for the file name in our handling of argc and argv. In the CP/M version we will have to do this.

Some examples of the command line structure will help:-

    grep the <file/one

This will search file/one for every occurrence of the word 'the'.

      grep -n the <file/one

Will search file/one for each occurrence of the word 'the' and the -n parameter specifies that we want the line number printed as well. There is one other parameter, this is -x, which means that we want all lines not containing the specified word. The parameters can be mixed:-

      grep -x -n the <file/one

Searches file/one for all lines not containing the word 'the' and prints out the corresponding line numbers.

```
/* Program 26 Grep in LC */
/* Written by Frank Shannon, Modified from Kernighan and Ritchie, Programming inC*/
#define MAXLINE 1000
#include STDIO/CSH
main (argc, argv) /* grep - find pattern from 1st arg */
int argc;
char *argv[];
{
  char line[MAXLINE], *s;
  int lineno, except, number;
  lineno = except = number = 0;
  while (--argc > 0 && (++argv) [0] == '-')
    {
      for (s = argv[0]+1; *s != '/0'; s++)
        switch (s) {
        case 'x':
          except = 1;
          break;
        case 'n':
          number = 1;
          break;
        default:
          printf("grep: illegal option %c. \n", *s);
          argc = 0;
          break;
                    }

      }
    if (argc != 1)
      printf("Usage: grep -x -n pattern <filen \n");
    else
      while (getline(line, MAXLINE) > 0)
        {
            lineno++;
            if ((index(line, *argv) >= 0) != except)
```

```
                {
                if (number)
                        printf("%d: ", lineno);
        printf("%s", line);
                }
            }
        }


getline(s, lim)                    /* get line into s, return length */
char s[];
int lim;
{
    int c, i;

    i = 0;
    while (--lim > 0 && (c=getchar()) != EOF && c != '\n')
       s[i++] = c;
    if (c == '\n')
       s[i++] = c;
    s[i] = '\0';
    return(i);
}


index(s, t)  /*return index of t in s, -1 if none */
char s[], t[];
{
   int i, j, k;
   for (i = 0; s[i] != '\0'; i++)
     {
       for (j=i, k=0; t[k]!='\0' && s[j]==t[k]; j++, k++)
       ;
        if (t[k] == '\0')
            return(i);
     }
   return(-1);
}
```

The program itself is divided into three functions. The first is main(argc,argv) and this contains the main body of the program. Function getline(s,lim) reads a line, from the specified file, into array s and returns its length. Function index(s,t) searches string s for the presence of string t. It returns the index of t in s if it is present, and if not it returns the value of -1.

The program begins with the usual definitions. Function main(argc,argv) starts by declaring argc and argv. Array line is the array that will hold the data read in from the input file. It is defined as having dimension [MAXLINE] where MAXLINE is 1000. This means that it sets the maximum number of input characters to 1000.

124

Variable s is a pointer to a character.

The three integer variables are declared and initialised in the usual way.

The control part of the while....loop states that the body of the loop is to be carried out while --argc is greater than zero and while the data pointed to by (++argv)[0] does not start with a '-' sign (remember the parameters above). The usage of the (++argv) [0] is new to us. It means that the first character pointed to by ++argv is to be tested. Quite simply the while loop will execute as long as argc is greater than zero and there are the option parameters present. Each time the loop is executed argc is decremented and argv is incremented.

The body of the loop consists of a for...loop which uses a switch..case construction to test for a number of conditions. The for..loop sets pointer s equal to argv[0]+1 (the second character pointed to by argv) and executes the switch....case section, incrementing the value of s by 1 each time. The loop terminates when s points to the value of '\0' meaning a blank character.

The for loop will be executed either once (for one optional parameter e.g. -n) twice (for both optional parameters eg -n -x) or no times (for no optional parameters). Should either of the optional parameters be entered then the variables "except" and "number" will be set. If these parameters are not entered then the variables will remain at their initial value of zero. If some unacceptable parameter was passed, then the warning message is printed and the value of argc is set to zero.

Once the while...loop is terminated a test is made for the value of argc. If this is not 1 (an error has been made) and the warning line is printed onto the screen. If argc is equal to 1 then all is well and the second part of the program begins.

This starts after the else statement with a while...loop. The control section of the loop repeatedly calls the getline function and continues the loop body while this function returns a string length. If zero is returned then the input file has been exhausted and the program terminates.

If a line has been read from the file then the line counter is incremented and the index function is called. This forms part of a complex function. The function is as follows:-

if((index(line, *argv) >=0) !=except)

We will have to look at this in some detail. Remember though since argv has been incremented throughout the first part of the program it now points to the data item we are searching with.

The test function breaks down into two parts. The first is the index(line, *argv) >=0 part. If the index(line, *argv) function returns an index position (*argv is in the line), then this section of code will be evaluated to 'true'. If data *argv is not in the line, then a value of -1 will be returned and the section of program will deliver a 'false' value.

As part of the standard #definitions 'true' is equivalent to 1 and 'false' is equivalent to 0. The value of this part of the function will now be tested against the != except part. This can have one of two values (1 if the -x parameter was specified and 0 otherwise). If it is 1 then we want the lines not containing data item *argv to be printed. If it is 0 then we want all the lines containing data item *argv to be displayed.

The following four possibilities exist:-

VALUE OF FUNCTION	VALUE OF EXCEPT	LINE PRINTED
1	1	no
1	0	yes
0	1	yes
0	0	no

In other words, if the function equates to 1 then the data has been found. If except is equal to 1, we don't want the line printed if the data is in it ..... and so on.

The final part of the program tests to see if the line number option was specified. If it was, and the above tests prove true, then the line number and the line are printed. If not, then the line is printed by itself.

Function getline(s, lim) simply inputs successive characters from the designated input file until one of the test conditions proves true. These test conditions are contained in the control section of the while...loop. The use of the --lim > 0 command means that the value of lim (passed to the function as MAXLINE) is decremented by 1 each time that the while...loop is executed. The loop will terminate when it is equal to zero (maximum input), or when the end of file is reached, or when a new line is input.

The reason that c=getchar() does not input from the keyboard is that the input redirection command has to be used to specify the input file. This redefines the getchar() function to input from this rather than from the keyboard. The remainder of this function loads array s with the input data. (Array s is the local variable equivalent of the data array line). When the termination conditions have been met, the last two characters of array s are set to '\n' and '\0' (new line and null) respectively. The function ends by returning the length of the string, obtained since the variable i was incremented each time the loop was executed.

The final function is index(s,t) which checks through the input string searching for the data item *argv. The two strings (line and *argv) are passed to the function and stored as local character arrays s and t. The central part of function index are two nested "for" loops.

The outer loop is for(i =0; s[i] != '\0'; i++) which simply steps through the array s until the end is reached. (this may be terminated by a return(i) statement if a match is found). The inner loop is another common but as yet unseen construction. Its structure is as follows:-

126

$$for(j=i,k=0;t[k]!='\backslash 0' \ \&\& \ s[j]==t[k]; \ j++,k++);$$

This loop starts with variables j and k set to their initial values and increments each one every time the loop is executed. By setting the value of j equal to i the main string will be worked through until a match is found. The inner loop will not start incrementing j and k until a match occurs. The inner loop can terminate due to one of two conditions. Either the end of string t has occurred (i.e. a match has been found) or s[j] is not equal to t[k]. If the termination condition is that string t has ended, then the value of i is returned. Otherwise a value of -1 is returned.

```
/* Program 25 modified for DeSmet C by K Sullivan*/
#define MAXLINE 1000
#define EOF -1
main (argc, argv) /* grep - find pattern from 1st arg */
int argc;
char *argv[];
{
  int fp;
  fp = fopen(argv[--argc],"r");
  char line[MAXLINE], *s;
  int lineno, except, number;
  lineno = except = number = 0;
  while (--argc > 0 && (++argv)[0] == '-')
    {
      for (s = argv[0]+1; *s != '\0'; s++)
      switch (s) {
      case 'x':
        except = 1;
        break;
      case 'n':
        number = 1;
        break;
      default:
        printf("grep: illegal option %c \n", *s);
        argc = 0;
        break;
                    }
    }
  if (argc != 1)
    printf("Usage: grep -x -n pattern filen \n");
    else
      while (getline(fp,line, MAXLINE) > 0)
        {
            lineno++;
            if ((index(line, *argv) >= 0) != except)
              {
                  if (number)
                      printf("%d: ", lineno);
```

```
                    printf("%s", line);
                }
        }
}

getline(ff,s, lim)  /* get line into s, return length */
int ff;
char s[];
int lim;
{
  int c, i;

  i = 0;
  while (--lim > 0 && (c=getchar()) != EOF && c != '\n')
     s[i++] = c;
  if (c == '\n')
     s[→++] = c;
  s[i] = '\0';
  return(i);
}

index(s, t)  /*return index of t in s, -1 if none */
char s[], t[];
{
  int i, j, k;
  for (i = 0; s[i] != '\0'; i++)
  {
    for (j=i, k=0; t[k]!='\0' && s[j]==t[k]; j++, k++)
       ;
    if (t[k] == '\0')
       return(i);
  }
  return(-1);
}
```

The main difference in the CP/M program is that an extra argument has to be passed due to the absence of any input/output redirection. This means that we have had to declare one extra variable (fp the file integer) and to open the file passed by argv[arc-1], or the last argument in the command line. The statement used to open the file is

        fp = fopen(argv[--argc],"r");

This serves two purposes. It opens the file that was specified and also decrements the value of argc so that it is the same for the rest of the program, just as if the extra argument had not been included. This minimises any other changes that we have to make.

These other changes are minimal. We have to remember to pass the value of fp when we call function getline(). This call is now as follows getline(fp,line,MAXLINE). Also since there is no input redirection we are unable to use the getchar() function. We have used c=getc(ff) in its place.

Apart from these minor changes, the program remains the same.

The use of the command line arguments argc and argv enable the programmer to construct a wide range of programs which are able to accept command line entries as part of their data structure. This means that it is possible to construct useful utilities and routines which can enhance the operating system in which C resides.

Summary of Chapter 9.

(1)   Introduction to command line arguments.

(2)   A simple example of the use of argc and argv.

(3)   Implementations of the UNIX utility GREP for both compilers.

Chapter 10

Structures.

This chapter deals with structures. These are collections of variables, often of different data types, but grouped together under a collective name for convenience in handling. They can represent a considerable simplification in the manipulation of complex data groups, but they are also one of the areas of the C language which is undergoing modification. Due to this, there is a great variation in the features available on C compilers for dealing with structures. One of our compilers does not support structures. The other only supports the 'standard' structure operations, not some of the later implementations of the language.

In this chapter we will introduce the basic concepts of structures and some of the more advanced methods of referencing and constructing them.

Program 26 illustrates some of the general principles behind structures.

```
/* Program 26 CP/M General structures */
#define EOF 3
struct dob {
    int day;
    char month[9];
    int year;
    };
struct dob g = { 4, "january", 1950 };
struct dob *f = &g;

main()
{
    scr.clr();
    printf("data is day %d month %s year %dn", f->day,f->month,f->year);
}
```

This program has one structure, called dob which consists of three variables, day (an integer), month (a character array), year (an integer). From this example, it can be seen that the variable declarations within the structure are the same as if they had been normal variable declarations.

The general syntax for a structure is as follows:-

```
struct NME {
        variable list;
        };
```

Where NME represents the structure name or tag, the position of the braces is not important, only their presence is.

Our structure dob contains three variables. Until the structure is initialised by assigning some data to it no storage will be allocated. The method that we will use to initialise a structure is illustrated by the line:-

```
struct dob g ={4, "january", 1950 };
```

This declares g to be a structure of type dob with the three variables assigned the values of 4, january, 1950. The order of the data in the list is important. The types must correspond to the variable types in the structure.

It is possible to declare pointers to structures. This is done in the next line which declares f to be a pointer to a structure of type dob. The value of f is set to the address of structure g in the same statement. We can now use this pointer to access the data in structure g.

The main program body consists of two lines. The first clears the screen and the second prints out each variable in the structure. The use of pointers is illustrated in this line. The general syntax for this operation is :-

```
pointer->member;
```

where member is a member of the structure in question and the -> operator means that the pointer refers to the member of the structure. The alternative method of referencing the individual members of a structure is shown below:-

```
      structure-name.member;
e.g.  dob.name;
      dob.year;
```

In these two simple examples the '.' operator is used to associate a structure name with a particular structure member. In the first example the statement dob.name means the member name in structure dob. To use the first type of reference the pointer must have been assigned to the structure in question.

It is possible to have arrays of structures. These can be useful for handling blocks of related data. Program 27 shows how this can be done.


```
/* Program 27 CP/M Arrays of Structures */
```

```
#define EOF 3
struct dob {
        char name[10];
        int day;
        char month[9];
        int year;
    };
struct dob book[7] = {
                "bill", 15, "january", 1936,
                "jane", 22, "march", 1948,
                "graham", 11, "april", 1961,
                "kevin", 23, "december", 1951,
                "ann", 18, "october", 1956,
                "mark", 28, "may", 1970,
                "ruth", 4, "october", 1971
                };


int c,i;

main()

{
    c = i = 1;
    while(!= EOF)
      {
            scr_clr();
            printf("which element of the table do you want to see ? \n");
            c = ci();
            c = c - '0';
            --c;
        if( c >= 7 )
            { printf("ERROR---------VALUE TOO HIGH \n");
                    break;
            }
            else
            {
                    printf("%-10s \n",book[c].name);
                    printf("%2d \n",book[c].day);
                    printf("%-8s \n",book[c].month);
                    printf("%4d \n",book[c].year);
            }
            scr_rowcol(10,0);
            printf("Type <CTRL-C> to end any other key to end \n");
            i = ci();

}
```

Program 27 uses the same structure as program 26 with one extra member. This

is a character array which will be used to store the name of the person in question.
It is declared to be an array of type "structure" by the statement:-

    struct dob book[7]

This means that book is a seven element array of type "structure", which conforms
to the construction of dob. We will then have seven occurrences of name, day,
month, year. The structure array is initialised in exactly the same way as before,
except that we now have far more data elements. Once again the order of the data
items is important. Each data item must match the structure member that it
corresponds to.

To illustrate the accessing of a structure array the function main() allows the user
to interrogate the array and prints the relevant data onto the screen. Much of this
function will be obvious, the two points worth noting are the conversion of the
ASCII value in variable c to an integer corresponding to the value of the key
pressed. This is done using the same techniques that were discussed in chapter 4.

The section which prints out the contents of the structures onto the screen uses a
series of printf() commands. The usual parameters have been set with the strings
being left justified. The method of accessing a particular element of the array is
shown in each of the printf() statements. The syntax is illustrated below:-

    structure-name[element].member;

The variable c contains the element number and the member required is indicated
in each of the printf() statements.

Continuing the overview of structures program 28 shows how it is possible to
create structures within structures. Not just that but arrays of structures within
structures.

```
/* Program 28 Structures within Structures */

#define EOF 3

struct abode {
        char road[21];
        char town[16];
        char phone[12];
        };
struct person {
        char name[21];
        char job[21];
        char dob[11];
        };

struct general {
```

```c
            struct person now;
            struct abode here;
            int worksn;
            int payno;
            int salary;
            char dept[31];
        } detail[6] = {
            "b. peters", "cleaner", "30/02/1970",
            "55 the road", "ilford", "111-1212",
            "1234, 9187, 5467, "maintenance",
            "r. jones", "dentist", "12/07/1952",
            "123 the avenue", "stratford", "121-2132",
            2315, 9621, 5684, "health",
            "k. smith", "lecturer", "27/01/48",
            "10 sunny street", "oxford", "19-2931",
            1425, 9172, 6487, "education",
            "p. healy", "electrician", "16/09/1962",
            "76 the drive", "leyton", "012-2341",
            2451, 9827, 5363, "maintenance",
            "k. hardy", "editor", "23/12/1948",
            "37 the westway", "bow", "435-1293",
            1534, 9273, 5464, "publishing",
            "n. bragg", "plumber", "23/10/1960",
            "92 walford road", "romford", "113-2931",
            2514, 9212, 5463, "maintenance",
        };

int a,b,c;


main()
{
    a = 1;
    while( a != EOF )
        {
            scr_clr();
            printf("There are six entries in the data table \n");
            printf("Please select your choice \n");
            c = ci();
            c = c - '0';
            if(c >= 7 ){ printf("ERROR ----- ENTRY NOT ACCEPTABLE \n");
break;}
--c;
scr_rowcol(5,0);
printf("Now select the <F>ull data or <P>art of the data \n");
b = ci();
scr_clr();
if(b == 'f' )
    {
```

```
                printf("FULL TABLE \n");
                printf("%-20s \n",detail[c].now.name);
                printf("%-20s \n",detail[c].now.job);
                printf("%-10s \n",detail[c].now.dob);
                printf("%-20s \n",detail[c].here.road);
                printf("%-15s \n",detail[c].here.town);
                printf("%-11s \n",detail[c].here.phone);
                printf("%d \n",detail[c].worksn);
                printf("%d \n",detail[c].payno);
                printf("%d \n",detail[c].salary);
                printf("%-30s \n",detail[c].dept);
            }
        else
            if(b == 'p')
                {
                    printf("PART TABLE \n");
                    printf("%-20s \n",detail[c].now.name);
                    printf("%-20s \n",detail[c].now.dob);
                    printf("%-11s \n".detail[c].here.phone);
                    printf("%-30s \n".detail[c].dept);
                }
            else
            printf("SORRY INCORRECT KEY \n");
        scr_rowcol(21,0);
        printf("Type <CTRL-C> to end any other key to continue \n");
        a = ci();
    }
}
```

In this example there is one primary structure and two sub-structures. The information contained in these structures is the sort that would be contained in an employer's payroll details. There is more information than the normal payroll requirements simply to illustrate the principles of complex structures.

The first structure is called abode and deals with the address of the employee. It contains three data items, all character arrays, called road, town, and phone. The second structure is called person and again contains three data items. These are name, job and dob(date of birth). Structure "general" is the principle structure and this declares the first two data items to be of type "structure". The structure declaration is the same as we have used before with the following syntax:-

                        struct struct-type name;

where struct-type refers to a particular pre-defined type of structure and name is an acceptable data name.

The next three data items are all integers with the following names:- worksn (works number), payno (payroll number) and salary. The method for declaring a structure array described in the previous section is used again to declare the

135

variable called detail as an arrayed structure of type general with six elements in the array.

The initialisation of the structure is of interest. It illustrates the fact that the structure is stored in memory as a block of data and manipulated by a series of pointers. All that we have done is to block together the relevant groups of data in the order in which structure "general" expects them.

This order is as follows:-

line 1   data items for structure person
line 2   data items for structure abode
line 3   data items for remainder of structure general

This pattern of data lines is then repeated, once for each element in the array.

The remainder of the program consists of the user 'interface' i.e. a series of program statements which allow the user to enter the array element that is to be displayed and the selection of either the full data or part of the full data.

The only point worth a more detailed discussion is the method of accessing the element in question. The hierarchial nature of 'structured' structures has to be considered. If we think of the structure array as a series of boxes we must go to the correct box (array element) that we have selected. Inside this box there are data items (the data items of structure detail and two other boxes (structures abode and person). These two sub-boxes can then be opened to access the data elements that they contain.

From this example the order of access is as follows:-

main structure->->-sub structure->->-data item

if the data item required is in the main structure then we can access it by the following method:-

main structure->->-data item

The following two pieces of program code illustrate these methods.

detail[c].now.name
detail[c].dept

This brings to an end our brief tour of structures. As was stated in the opening paragraph there is a great deal of variation in the ways that different compilers have utilised the various structure implementations in C. No doubt as time goes on more and more of these will approach the latest developments in structure manipulation. For the time being it is best to stick with the smallest common sub-set of structure commands and manipulations, to keep program portability.

Summary of Chapter 10.

(1)   Introduction to structures, structure declaration and initialisation.

(2)   Pointers to structures and structure accessing.

(3)   Arrays of structures, declaration initialisation and accessing.

(4)   Structures of structures, declaration, initialisation and accessing.

Chapter 11

Sorting & Sorting methods

The final chapter in the book deals with one of the perennial problems of the computer industry, that of sorting data. While some of the simpler techniques can be perfectly adequate for small blocks of regular data the problem rapidly becomes complex when dealing with the size of data found in commercial and business applications.

We will look at two programs, one is an internal sorting program (one which sorts a data block small enough to fit in the computer's memory) and the other is an external sorting program (one which sorts a file that is too large to fit inside the computer's memory). Sorting and sort methods is a very specialised area of computing and is one which could be (in fact is) the subject of a book in its own right. We will explain some of the background to the first sorting method used. The reader is referred to some of the more advanced texts for a detailed discussion of the other methods and sorting techniques in general.

The first program uses a sorting method called the Shell sort. This was named after D.L. Shell who first described the technique in 1959. The whole development of sorting techniques is based around gradual modifications and improvements to existing techniques. The method used to illustrate the Shell sort is one way of implementing the general algorithm. There are a great deal of others.

The Shell sort starts by comparing all elements which are n/2 elements apart. Strictly speaking these are the integer value of n/2, to cover the occasions where the number of data elements (n) is odd. If the data pair that is compared is not ordered then they are exchanged.

The technique can be illustrated by means of the following list of data.

9, 11, 4, 13, 6, 3, 5, 12, 7, 8, 4, 10

There are twelve data elements and so the range of the comparisons is six. This means that element one will be compared with element seven, element two with element eight and so on. The following table will help to make this clear.

First half of table	Second half of table	Exchange made
9	5	yes
11	12	no
4	7	no
13	8	yes
6	4	yes
3	10	no

In each case the data item in the first half of the table is compared with the corresponding item in the second half of the table. If the second is smaller than the first then an exchange is made.

Once this first pass is made then the two parts are combined. This produces the following data list:-

5, 11, 4, 8, 4, 3, 9, 12, 7, 13, 6, 10

For the second phase the gap is again halved (giving us a gap length of three). This means that element one will be compared with element four, element two with element five etc. The list above is now broken down into the required number of sub sets as shown in the following table:-

1st list	2nd list	3rd list	4th list	exchanged
5	8	9	13	no
11	4	12	6	yes
4	3	7	10	no

The comparisons made in this phase are rather more complex than those in the initial phase of the sort. In the second line (the only one in which exchanges are made) the following sequence of events would take place:-

list of data items		items compared	exchanged
11, 4, 12, 6		11 & 4	yes
4, 11, 12, 6		11 & 12	no
4, 11, 12, 6		12 & 6	yes
4, 11, 6, 12	*sec	11 & 6	yes
4, 6, 11, 12	*sec	4 & 6	no
4, 6, 11, 12		none	-----

The comparison marked *sec is called a secondary comparison since it follows a primary exchange which modifies the order of the list, created by an earlier exchange. If the sorting technique used did not keep track of these then a faulty sort would result.

The numbers are then merged to produce the following (almost sorted list).

5, 4, 3, 8, 6, 4, 9, 11, 7, 13, 12, 10

Using the same techniques as above the gap is now reduced to the integer of 3/2 (the old gap halved). This gives a value of 1 and so represents the final gap length. Since all of the 'long distance' data moves have been done only relatively short distance exchanges now take place. By the principles of exchanging and merging the final sorted list is produced.

3, 4, 4, 5, 6, 7, 8, 9, 10, 11, 12, 13

Our example program uses the Shell sort method as its sorting routine. Since we are dealing with text data we have another problem to overcome. One of the main problems with sorting such data is the fact that the moves corresponding to data exchanges can themselves take a considerable amount of time. One way of overcoming this is not to sort the data items themselves but to sort a table of pointers to the data items.

Since these pointers can be stored as integer quantities it then means that we only have to exchange a table of integer values (a far faster operation than text data moves). This technique is employed in program 29 .

```
/* Program 29 Shell Sort written for LC by Larry Richards*/
#include stdio/csh
#option INLIB
#define MAXLEN 255
#define LINES 2000 /* max lines to be sorted */ main()
{
  int *lineptr[LINES];
  int nlines;
  unsigned i;
  printf("Memory free: %u bytes \n",freemem());
  if ((nlines = readlines(lineptr, LINES)) >=0)
  {
    sort(lineptr, nlines);
    writelines(lineptr, nlines);
    exit(0);
  }
  else
    printf("input too big to sort \n");
    exit(0);
}
```

```
readlines(lineptr, maxlines)
int *lineptr[];
int maxlines;
{
  int len, nlines;
  char line[MAXLEN];
  int p;
  nlines = 0;
  while ((len = getline(line, MAXLEN)) >0)
    if (nlines >= maxlines)
      return(-1);
    else if ((p = alloc(len)) == NULL)
      return(-1);
    else {
      line[len-1] = '\0';
      strcpy(p,line);
      lineptr[nlines++] = p;
    }
  return(nlines);
}
writelines(lineptr,nlines)
int *lineptr[];
int nlines;
{
  int i;
  for (i=0; i< nlines; i++)
    printf("%s",lineptr[i]);
}
sort(v,n)
char *v[];
int n;
{
  int gap, i, j;
  int *temp;
  for (gap = n/2; gap > 0; gap /=2)
    for (i=gap; i <n; i++)
      for (j=i-gap; j >=0; j-= gap)
      { if (strcmp(v[j], v[j+gap]) <=0)
          break;
        temp = v[j];
        v[j] = v[j+gap];
        v[j+gap] = temp;
      }
}
getline(s,lim)
char s[];
int lim;
{
  int c, i;
  i = 0;
```

141

```
while (--lim >0 && (c=getchar()) != eof && c != ' \ n')
  s[i++] = c;
if (c == ' \n')
  s[i++] = c;
s[i] = ' \0';
  return(i);
}
```

Program 29 consists of four functions. The first is main() which calls the other routines, sets up some of the parameters and prints out warning messages. The data items used in this section of the program are as follows:-

int *lineptr[LINES]   An array of pointers to the data items held in memory.

int nlines   An integer variable holding the number of lines read in.

The printf() function checks the available free memory by use of the freemem() statement and then prints out the amount of memory. This is a 'cosmetic' procedure which has no effect on the running of the system.

The next statement is a compound expression which checks the value assigned to nlines by the function call readlines(lineptr, LINES). If this is greater than or equal to zero then the sort routine is called. Otherwise the warning message is printed and the program terminates.

Function readlines(lineptr, maxlines) uses the same variables as function main but declares them with different local names. It declares three local integers, len, lines and p together with a local character array line[MAXLEN]. The variable nlines is set equal to zero and another function call is made.

This calls function getline(line, MAXLEN) which inputs the data from the file specified by the input/output redirection provided at the command line. The parameters passed to this function are for the character array line[] and for the maximum length of a line (declared at the start of the program).

Function getline() uses a character array c[] to store the incoming data and an integer lim to store the maximum number of lines. The program consists of a single while...... loop which inputs each character from the file in question and checks to see (1) if the line length is acceptable (--lim >0) (2) if the end of the file has been reached (!=eof) (3) is the character just input a new line (!='\n'). If any of these conditions is met then the while....loop terminates. As long as these conditions are met (i.e. the character just input is acceptable) then it is entered into the array s[i++]. Should this input routine be terminated then the statement if(c == '\n') checks to see if the last character was an end of line (new line). If this was so then the next element in s is set equal to the new line character and the element after is set to the null character. The length of the string (contained in integer i) is returned to the calling function by the normal method.

The value returned by the getline() function is tested to see if it is greater than zero. If it is, then two further tests are carried out. The first checks to see if nlines is greater then the maximum number of lines allowed in the program. If the test evaluates to true then too many lines have been read in and the function returns a value of -1.

The second test checks to see if the memory allocation routine returns a null value (if insufficient memory is available then this will occur). If this test is true then a value of -1 is returned. In both of the above cases, the calling function will test for the presence of a -1 as an indicator of an error condition.

Assuming that there is sufficient memory and that the number of lines read in is acceptable then the element, one from last, is set equal to the null character. This has the effect of removing the new line character. The character array is then copied into the memory location indicated by p. The value of p is then stored into the array of pointers to the text lines. The above actions are carried out by the following three lines:-

```
line[len-1] = '\0';
strcpy(p,line);
lineptr[nlines++] = p;
```

The final statement also increments the value of nlines for both the test inside the while......loop and so that it will point to the correct location if another line is read in.

The function then returns the value of the number of lines to the function main(). At this point in the program the array lineptr[] contains the memory locations of all of the text lines read in from the input file. The variable nlines contains the number of lines to be sorted.

Should the returned value (from function readlines()) be greater than or equal to zero the sort function is called. If a value of -1 was returned then the error message is printed out and the program execution terminated.

The sort routine is called by the function call sort(lineptr, nlines). This passes the parameters lineptr and nlines to the sort function. Remember that lineptr is an array of pointers to the data read in by function readlines(). The integer variable lines tells the function sort() how many lines of text there are to sort. The sort routine is an implementation of the Shell sort algorithm described above. The gap calculated is the result of an integer division of n (the number of lines) by 2. Most of the routine is self explanatory. The three nested for...loops make the routine tricky to follow. Should this prove too complex, the only way to understand the routine properly is to trace it through with some dummy data. To understand the way in which the program functions, it is only necessary to have a rough understanding of this particular sort routine.

Once the data has been sorted the function writelines() prints the lines pointed to by the sorted array linptr[] onto the screen. Clearly this could be modified to copy the data back onto a 'sorted data' disk file. This is done in the CP/M version of the program.

```
/* Program 29 CP/M Shell Sort modified for DeSmet C */
/* by K. Sullivan.*/
#define stdin 0
#define NULL 0
#define EOF -1
#define MAXLEN 255
#define LINES 2000 /* max lines to be sorted */
main()
{
int *lineptr[LINES];
  int ges, nlines;
  char *tm, *bm;
  clear();
  file name();
  fi = fopen(&e[0], "r");
  fo = fopen(&f[0], "w");
  tm = showsp();
  bm = memory();
  printf("Memory free: %u bytes \n",(tm-bm));
  printf("Type any key to continue \n");
  ges = ci();
  if ((nlines = readlines(lineptr, LINES)) >=0)
  {
    sort(lineptr, nlines);
    writelines(lineptr, nlines);
    exit(0);
}
else
    printf("input too big to sort \n");
    exit(0);
}
readlines(lineptr, maxlines)
int *lineptr[];
int maxlines;
{
    int len, nlines;
    char line[MAXLEN];
    int p;
    nlines = 0;
    while ((len = getline(line, MAXLEN)) >0)
  if (nlines >= maxlines)
     return(-1);
    else if ((p = malloc(len)) == NULL)
     return(-1);
    else {
    line[len-1] = ' \0';
    strcpy(p,line);
    lineptr[nlines++] = p;
    }
```

```c
    return(nlines);
}
writelines(lineptr,nlines)
int *lineptr[];
int nlines;
{
  int i;
  for (i=0; i< nlines; i++)
    printf("%s",lineptr[i]);
    fprintf(fo,"%s",lineptr[i]);
}
sort(v,n)
char *v[];
int n;
{
  register int gap, i, j;
  int *temp;
  for (gap = n/2; gap > 0; gap /=2)
    for (i=gap; i <n; i++)
      for (j=i-gap; j >=0; j-= gap)
      { if (strcmp(v[j], v[j+gap]) <=0)
        break;
        temp = v[j];
        v[j] = v[j+gap];
        v[j+gap] = temp;
      }
}
getline(s,lim)
  char s[];
int lim;
{
  clear();
  printf("READING THE FILE \n");
  int c, i;
  i = 0;
  while (--lim >0 && (c=getc(fi)) != EOF && c != 10)
    s[i++] = c;
  if (c == 10)
    s[i++] = 10;
  s[i] = '\0';
  if(i==0)return(0);
      else
        return(i);
}

clear()
{
    scr_clr();
    scr_rowcol(0,0);
```

145

```
    }

file name()
{
    -setmem(&e[0],30,0);
    -setmem(&f[0],30,0);
    clear();
    printf("Please enter the name of the file to be read \n");
    fgets(&e[0],15,stdin);
    sl = strlen(&e[0]);
    e[sl] = 0x0a;
    clear();
    printf("Please enter the name of the file for the OUTPUT \");
    fgets(&f[0],15,stdin);
    sl = strlen(&f[0]);
    f[sl] = 0x0a;
    clear();
}

finish()
{
    fclose(fi);
    fclose(fo);
    exit(0);
}
```

The main difference between this program and the original program 29 is that this one outputs the sorted data into another disk file, named by the user. There are other differences in the method of determining the amount of memory available. The DeSmet compiler uses two functions, one to test for the top of available memory, the other to test for the bottom of available memory. The difference between the two gives the amount of memory available to the user.

For some reason the DeSmet compiler refused to test for the '\n' character if it was expressed in the previous form. By converting this to the decimal form of the same character the problem was solved.

Apart from the addition of the extra functions needed to produce a working disk access program (remember there is no input/output redirection in this compiler/ operating system), the essential features of the program remain the same. The main limiting factor on this type of sort is the disk access times. By adding a disk write routine (only one extra line in function writelines(),) the overall times for the sort were increased quite considerably. Once again this illustrates the compromise between maximising the speed of the overall program and maximising its usefulness as a utility.

Our next program example is a much more sophisticated beast and involves a relatively complex sort/merg program.


```
/*Program 30*/
/*   SORTMRG /CCC   Sort/Merge from Software Tools by Kernighan &
     Plauger Converted from RATFOR to BDS C by Leor Zolman Sep 2, 1982
     Usage: sort <infile> <outfile>
     Main variables have been made external; this is pretty much in line with the
     RATFOR call-by-name convention anyway.
     Requires lots of disk space, up to about twice the space of the file being
     sorted. */
/*        Converted from BDS C to LC by Tom Sellers Dec 23, 1982 Modified to
     merge to output file on last pass rather than TEMP file.
     Modified to bypass the merge phase if the sort can be completed in memory
     alone. In this case only additional disk space for the sorted output file is required.
     The merge phase requires an additional amount of temporary disk space at least
     equal in size to the input file. The temporary files have names such as
     TEMP1/TMP:1 TEMP2/TMP:1 ..., so ensure that these names do not conflict
     with filenames already in use.
        If fgets() is altered to return \n, change the line in gtext() from
        lbp += (len + 1); ** drop '\n' ...
     to
        linbuf [lbp + len - 1] = '\0'; ** put \0 on top of \n
        lbp += len;    **drop ' \n', but keep NULL at string end
*/
#include STDIO/CSH
#option inlib
#option FIXBUFS ON
#option ZVAR ON
#define ERROR 0
#define MAXTEXT 20000  /* Size of text sort buffer */
#define MAXLINE 200 /* longest line we want to deal with */
#define MAXPTR 1500  /* Max number of lines */
#define MAXPTR1 1501
#define MRGORDER 7  /* Max # of intermediate files to merge */
#define MRGORDR1   8  /* Max # files open at one time */
#define LOGPTR  13 /* smallest value >= log (base 2) of
MAXPTR */
#define LOGPTR1  14
char name[13], name2[23]; /* TEMP filenames */
FILE *infil[MRGORDR1];  /* Array of file pointers for work files
*/
FILE *infile, *outfile, *tmpfile;
unsigned linptr[MAXPTR1], nlines;
int  temp;
char *linbuf, endext[MAXTEXT]; /* pointer to, &, sort buffer */
  /* If MAXTEXT is too large, KILL TEMPn/TMP:1 doesn't
    have enough room to work */
```

147

```
main(argc,argv)
int  argc;
char *argv[];
{
  unsigned high, lim, low, t;
  linbuf = endext; /* assign pointer to sort buffer */
  if (argc < 3)
    exit(puts("Usage: sort <infile> <outfile>\n"));
  if ((infile = fopen(argv[1],"R")) == ERROR)
    {
    printf("Can't open %s\n", argv[1]);
    exit(-1);
    }
  puts("Beginning initial formation run\n");
  high = 0;   /* Initial formation of runs: */
  do {
    t = gtext(infile);
    if (nlines == 0)
      break;
    quick(nlines);
if (t == 0 && high == 0)  /* file fits in memory */
    tmpfile = fopen(argv[2],"W"); /* write to output file */
    else
      {
      high++;
      tmpfile = makfil(high);  /* make new file n */
      }
    ptext(tmpfile);
    fclose(tmpfile);
  } while (t != NULL);
  fclose(infile);   /* free up the input file buffer */
  if (high != 0)   /* test if we need the merge now */
  {
    puts("Beginning merge operation\n");
    for (low = 1; low < high; low += MRGORDER)  /* merge */
  {
    lim = min(low = MRGORDER - 1, high);
    gopen(low, lim);   /* open files */
    if ((high - low) < MRGORDER) /* if no more than MRGORDER */
      tmpfile = fopen(argv[2],"W"); /* files remaining,  */
                /* merge to the output file */
      else
        {
        high++;
        tmpfile = makfil(high);
        }
      merge(lim - low + 1, tmpfile);
      fclose(tmpfile); /* close merge output TEMP file */
        gremov(low, lim);
```

```
    }
    fclose(outfile);
  }
}

/*
*
*/
Quick: Quicksort for character lines
*/
quick(nlines)
unsigned nlines;
{
  unsigned i,j, lv[LOGPTR1], p, pivlin, uv[LOGPTR1];
  int compar();
  lv[1] = 1;
  uv[1] = nlines;
  p = 1;
  while (p > 0)
   if (lv[p] >= uv[p]) /* only 1 element in this subset */
     p--; /* pop stack */
   else
     {
     i = lv[p] - 1;
     j = uv[p];
     pivlin = linptr[j]; /* pivot line */
     while (i < j)
       {
          for (i++; compar(linptr[i],pivlin) < 0; i++)
        ;
          for (j--; j > i; j--)
        if (compar(linptr[j], pivlin) <= 0)
          break;
          if (i < j) /* out of order pair */
            {
        temp = linptr[i];
        linptr[i] = linptr[j];
        linptr[j] = temp;
            }
       }
     j = uv[p]; /* move pivot to position 1 */
     temp = linptr[i];
     linptr[i] = linptr[j];
     linptr[j] = temp;
     if ( (i - lv[p]) < (uv[p] - i))
        {
        lv[p + 1] = lv[p];
        uv[p + 1] = i - 1;
        lv[p] = i + 1;
        }
     else
```

```
         {
      lv[p + 1] = i + 1;
      uv[p + 1] = uv[p];
      uv[p] = i - 1;
         }
      p++;
         }
    return;
}
/*
   * Compar: Compare two strings; return 0 if equal, -1 if first is
   *    lexically smaller, or 1 if first is bigger
   */
compar(lp1, lp2)
unsigned lp1, lp2;
{
   unsigned i, j;
   for (i = lp1, j = lp2; linbuf[i] == linbuf[j]; i++,j++)
     if (linbuf[i] == ' \0') /* Test end of string */
        return 0;
   return (linbuf[i] < linbuf[j]) ? -1 : 1;
}
/*
   * Ptext: output text lines from linbuf using the pointer to output line
   */
ptext(outfil)
FILE *outfil;
   {
     int i;
     for (i = 1; i <= nlines; i++) {
        if (fputs(&linbuf[linptr[i]], outfil) == EOF) {
        puts("Error writing output file..disk full? \n");
          exit(-1);
        }
        /*putc('\n', outfil);  terminate the line */
}
   return 0;
}
/*
   * Gtext: Get text lines from the buffered input file provided, and
   *    place them into linbuf
   */
gtext(infile)
FILE *infile;
{
   unsigned lbp, len;
   nlines = 0;
   lbp = 1;
   do {
     if (len = fgets(&linbuf[lbp],MAXLINE,infile) == NULL)
          return (0);
```
150

```
    len = strlen(&linbuf[lbp]);
    nlines++;
    linptr[nlines] = lbp;
    lbp += (len + 1);  /* drop '\n', but keep NULL at end of string */
  } while ( lbp < (MAXTEXT - MAXLINE) && nlines < MAXPTR);
  return (len);  /* return 0 if done with file */
}
/*
 * Makfil: Make a temporary file having suffix 'n' and open it for output
 */
makfil(n)   /* make temp file having suffix 'n' */
int n;
{
  FILE *obuf;
  char name[20];
  gname(n,name);
  if ((obuf = fopen(name,"W")) == ERROR) {
    printf("Can't create %s \n", name);
    exit(-1);
  }
  return (obuf);              /*file pointer to output buffer */
}
/*
 * Gname: Make temporary filename with suffix 'n/TMP:1'
 */
gname(n,name)
char *name;
int n;
{
  char tmptext[10];
  strcpy(name,"TEMP");.          /* create "TEMPn/TMP"  */
  itoa(n,tmptext);
  strcat(name,tmptext);
  strcat(name,"/TMP:4");
  return name;  /* return a pointer to it */
}
/*
 * Gopen: open group of files low...lim
 */
gopen(low, lim)
int lim, low;
{
  int i;
  printf("Opening temp files %d-%d \n",low,lim);
  for (i = 1; i <= (lim - low + 1); i++)
  {
    gname(low + i - 1, name);
    if ((infil[i] = fopen(name,"R")) == ERROR)
    {
```

```c
        puts("Can't open: "); puts(name); exit(-1);;
     }
   }
}
/*
 * Remove group of files low...lim
 */
gremov(low, lim)
int lim, low;
{
  int i;
  printf("Removing temp files %d-%d \n",low,lim);
  for (i = 1; i <= (lim - low + 1); i++)
{
    gname(low + i - 1, name);
    fclose(infil[i]);
    unlink(name);  /* kill the work files */
    }
}
/*
 * Merge: merge infil[1]...infil[nfiles] onto outfil
 */
merge(nfiles, outfil)
unsigned nfiles;
FILE *outfil;
{
  int i, inf, lbp, lp1, nf;
  lbp = 1;
  nf = 0;
  for (i = 1; i <= nfiles; i++)  /* get one line from each file */
    if (fgets(&linbuf[lbp],MAXLINE, infil[i]) != NULL)
    {
      nf++;
      linptr[nf] = lbp;
      lbp += MAXLINE; /* leave room for largest line */
    }
  quick(nf);  /* make initial heap */
  while (nf > 0) {
    lp1 = linptr[1];
    fputs(&linbuf[lp1], outfil);
    /*putc(' \n', outfil);*/
      nf = lp1 / MAXLINE + 1; /* compute file index */
    if (fgets(&linbuf[lp1],MAXLINE,infil[inf]) == NULL)
    {
          linptr[1] = linptr[nf];
          nf--;
    }
    reheap(nf);
    }
```

```
      return;
}
/*
  * Reheap: propagate linbuf[linptr[1]] to proper place in heap
  */
reheap(nf)
unsigned nf;
{
  unsigned i,j;
  for (i = 1; (i = i) <= nf; i = j)
  {
    j = i +i;
    if (j < nf) /* find smaller child */
          if (compar(linptr[j],linptr[j+1]) > 0)
        j++;
    if (compar(linptr[i], linptr[j]) <= 0)
      break;  /* Now at proper location */
    temp = linptr[i]; /* percolate */
    linptr[i] = linptr[j];
    linptr[j] = temp;
  }
  return;
}
/*
min   return the smaller of two values
*/
min(val1,val2)
unsigned int val1,val2;
{
        if (val1 < val2)
  return (val1);
  else
  return (val2);
}
/*
  * Unlink: kill the named file
  */
unlink(name)
{
  int retcod;
  strcpy(name2,"KILL ");
  strcat(name2,name);
  retcod = cmd(name2);    /* kill the file */
  return;
}
```

This final program consists of the following thirteen functions:-

main()	quick()	compar()
ptext()	gtext()	makfil()
gname()	gopen()	gremov()
merge()	reheap()	min()
unlink()		

As was stated at the start of the chapter we will not be looking at this program in great detail. Some of the more interesting aspects will be pointed out, but it is left up to the individual reader to trace through sections of code wherever necessary to get a feel for how the program works.

Function main() starts by declaring all the relevant variables and arrays. It opens the input file using the argv[1] array to hold the command line data. If this file is opened successfully then a call is made to gtext(), passing the value of the file pointer to this function.

Function gtext() is very similar to the function readlines() in our previous program. What it does is to read the data into a buffer linbuf[], and the accompanying pointers to the relevant addresses of each data block into the array linptr[]. The local variables lbp and len hold the values of the current block address and the length of the current block respectively. The global variables nlines, linptr[] and linbuf[] hold the values of the number of lines read, the addresses of those lines and the lines themselves. The body of this function consists of a do....while loop which terminates when the file is at an end, or when the maximum block of data has been read in.

Briefly, the program will read in the file in blocks if it is too large to fit into memory. If this is the case, then the blocks will be sorted and written out to the temporary files, which will be removed at the end of the sort. The temporary files hold sorted blocks of text which have to be merged to produce a final fully sorted file.

The method of creating the temporary files is quite ingenious. Firstly function makfil() is called and the value n is passed to it. This contains the reference number of the file in question. (in this way the first file will have a reference number of 1, the second 2, and so on). Function makfil() then declares the file pointer and a 20 element character array, that will be used to hold the files name. Once these have been declared the function gname() is called.

This function actually creates the temporary files name by a series of string manipulation commands. The first action is to copy the temporary file suffix "TEMP" into the array name. This is done using the strcpy statement. Then the function itoa() is used to convert the integer value of the variable n into the character string equivalent. This character string is held in the array tmptext[], which is then concatenated (joined) to the array name[] to produce a combined array which is the temporary file name.

Once this file name has been created the file is opened and the data written to it.

Function compar() is called to compare the two blocks of data pointed to by the integers lp1 and lp2. These are actually the current values of the pointer array linptr[]. The central part of this function is a for....loop which steps through the two data blocks as long as the present two characters are equal. The function is exited under one of three conditions. (1) if linbuf[i] is equal to ' O' then the end of a string has been found and the two strings are equal. Otherwise the strings must be different. (2) using the '?:' construction seen earlier if linbuf[i] is less than linbuf[j] then the value of -1 is returned. (3) if linbuf[i] is greater than linbuf[j] then a value of 1 is returned.

Two points to remember are that the array linbuf[] is a global array and therefore can be accessed from any function in the program without being redefined.

Function quick() uses a more advanced sorting routine than the Shell sort one that was described earlier. The reader is referred to a more advanced text on sorting for a detailed description of this routine.

```
/* Program 30 CP/M */
/*    SORTMRG /CCC   Sort/Merge from Software Tools by Kernighan &
      Plauger Converted from RATFOR to BDS C by Leor Zolman Sep 2, 1982
      Usage: sort <infile> <outfile>
      Converted to DeSmet C by K Sullivan Feb 12 1984
      Main variables have been made external; this is pretty much in line with the
      RATFOR call-by-name convention anyway.
      Requires lots of disk space, up to about twice the space of the file being
      sorted. */
/*        Converted from BDS C to LC by Tom Sellers Dec 23, 1982
   Modified to merge to output file on last pass rather than TEMP file.
   Modified to bypass the merge phase if the sort can be completed in memory
   alone. In this case only additional disk space for the sorted output file is required.
   The merge phase requires an additional amount of temporary disk space at least
   equal in size to the input file. The temporary files have names such as
   B:TEMP1/TMP B:TEMP2/TMP ..., so ensure that these names do not conflict
   with filenames already in use.
   If fgets() is altered to return \n, change the line in gtext() from
      lbp += (len + 1); ** drop '\n' ...
   to
      linbuf[lbp + len - 1] = '\0'; ** put \0 on top of \n
      lbp += len;   **drop '\n', but keep NULL at string end
*/
#define ERROR 0
#define MAXTEXT 20000  /* Size of text sort buffer */
#define MAXLINE 200 /* longest line we want to deal with */
#define MAXPTR 1500  /* Max number of lines */
#define MAXPTR1 1501
#define MRGORDER 7  /* Max # of intermediate files to merge */
#define MRGORDR1   8  /* Max # files open at one time */
#define LOGPTR  13 /* smallest value >= log (base 2) of MAXPTR */
#define LOGPTR1   14
#define EOF -1
#define NULL 0
```

```c
char name [13], name2[23]; /* TEMP filenames*/
int infil[MRGORDR1];  /* Array of file pointers for work files */
int  infile, outfile, tmpfile;
unsigned linptr[MAXPTR1], nlines;
int  temp;
char *linbuf, endext[MAXTEXT]; /* pointer to, &, sort buffer */
    /* If MAXTEXT is too large, KILL TEMPn/TMP:1 doesn't
      have enough room to work */

main(argc,argv)
int  argc;
char *argv[];
{
  unsigned high, lim, low, t;
  linbuf = endext; /* assign pointer to sort buffer */
  if (argc < 3)
     {
       puts("Usage: sort <infile> <outfile> \n");
       exit(0);
     }

  if ((infile = fopen(argv[1],"R")) == ERROR)
     {
     printf("Can't open %s/n", argv[1]);
     exit(-1);
     }
  puts("Beginning initial formation run \n");
  high = 0;   /* Initial formation of runs: */
  do {
    t = gtext(infile);
    if (nlines == 0)
      break;
    quick(nlines);
  if (t == 0 && high == 0)  /* file fits in memory */
      tmpfile = fopen(argv[2],"W"); /* write to output file */
    else
      {
      high++;
      tmpfile = makfil(high);  /* make new file n */
      }
    ptext(tmpfile);
    fclose(tmpfile);
  } while (t != NULL);
  fclose(infile);   /* free up the input file buffer */
  if (high != 0)    /* test if we need the merge now */
{
    puts("Beginning merge operation/n");
    for (low = 1; low < high; low <= MRGORDER)  /* merge */
{
```

```
        lim = min(low + MRGORDER - 1, high);
        gopen(low, lim);    /* open files */
        if ((high - low) < MRGORDER) /* if no more than MRGORDER */
          tmpfile = fopen(argv[2],"W"); /* files remaining, */
                    /* merge to the output file */
      else
        {
        high++;
      tmpfile = makfil(high);
        }
      merge(lim - low + 1, tmpfile);
      fclose(tmpfile); /* close merge output TEMP file */
        gremov(low, lim);
      }
      fclose(outfile);
  }
}

/*
 * Quick: Quicksort for character lines
 */
quick(nlines)
register unsigned nlines;
{
  unsigned i,j, lv[LOGPTR1], p, pivlin, uv[LOGPTR1];
  int compar();
  lv[1] = 1;
  uv[1] = nlines;
  p = 1;
  while (p > 0)
    if (lv[p] >= uv[p]) /* only 1 element in this subset */
      p--;  /* pop stack   */
    else
      {
      i = lv[p] - 1;
      j = uv[p];
      pivlin = linptr[j]; /* pivot line  */
      while (i < j)
        {
          for (i++; compar(linptr[i],pivlin) < 0; i++)
          ;
          for (j--; j > i; j--)
          if (compar(linptr[j], pivlin) <= 0)
          break;
          if (i < j) /* out of order pair */
          {
          temp = linptr[i];
          linptr[i] = linptr[j];
          linptr[j] = temp;
            }
```

157

```c
        }
    j = uv[p]; /* move pivot to position 1 */
    temp = linptr[i];
    linptr[i] = linptr[j];
    linptr[j] = temp;
    if ( (i - lv[p]) < (uv[p] - i))
        {
        lv[p + 1] = lv[p];
        uv[p + 1] = i - 1;
        lv[p] = i + 1;
        {
    else
        }
        lv[p + 1] = i + 1;
        uv[p + 1] = uv[p];
        uv[p] = i - 1;
        }
    p++;
    }
    return;
}
/*
 * Compar: Compare two strings; return 0 if equal, -1 if first is
 *    lexically smaller, or 1 if first is bigger
 */
compar(lp1, lp2)
unsigned lp1, lp2;
{
    register unsigned i, j;
    for (i = lp1, j = lp2; linbuf[i] == linbuf[j]; i++,j++)
        if (linbuf[i] == ' \0') /* Test end of string */
            return 0;
    return (linbuf[i] < linbuf[j]) ? -1 : 1;
}
/*
 * Ptext: output text lines from linbuf using the pointer to output line
 */
ptext(outfil)
int outfil;
{
    register int i;
    for (i = 1; i <= nlines; i++) {
        if (fputs(&linbuf[linptr[i]], outfil) == EOF) {
        puts("Error writing output file..disk full? \n");
        exit(-1);
        }
        /*putc(' \n', outfil);  terminate the line */
    }
    return 0;
```

```
}
/*
 * Gtext: Get text lines from the buffered input file provided, and
 *   place them into linbuf
 */
gtext(infile)
int infile;
{
  unsigned lbp, len;
  nlines = 0;
  lbp = 1;
  do {
    if (len = fgets(&linbuf[lbp],MAXLINE,infile) == NULL)
         return (0);
    len = strlen(&linbuf[lbp]);
    nlines++;
    linptr[nlines] = lbp;
    lbp += (len + 1); /* drop '\n', but keep NULL at end of string */
  } while ( lbp < (MAXTEXT - MAXLINE) && nlines < MAXPTR);
  return (len);  /* return 0 if done with file */
}
/*
 * Makfil: Make a temporary file having suffix 'n' and open it for output
 */
makfil(n)   /* make temp file having suffix 'n' */
int n;
{
  int obuf;
  char name[20];
  gname(n,name);
  if ((obuf = fopen(name,"W")) == ERROR) {
    printf("Can't create %s \n", name);
    exit(-1);
  }
  return (obuf);/*file pointer to output buffer */
}
/*
 * Gname: Make temporary filename with suffix 'n/TMP:1'
 */
gname(n,name)
char *name;
int n;
{
  char tmptext[10];
  strcpy(name,"B:TEMP");             /* create "TEMPn/TMP"     */
  itoa(n,tmptext);
  strcat(name,tmptext);
  strcat(name,".TMP");
  return name;     /* return a pointer to it */
```

```
}
/*
 *Gopen: open group of files low...lim
 */
gopen(low,lim)
int lim, low;
{
  int i;
  printf("Opening temp files %d-%d\n",low,lim);
  for (i = 1; i <= (lim - low + 1); i++)
  {
    gname(low + i - 1, name);
    if ((infil[i] = fopen(name,"R")) == ERROR)
    {
      puts("Can't open: "); puts(name); exit(-1);;
    }
  }
}
/*
 * Remove group of files low...lim
 */
gremov(low, lim)
int lim, low;
{
  int i;
  printf("Removing temp files %d-%d\n",low,lim);
  for (i = 1; i <= (lim - low + 1); i++)
  {
    gname(low + i - 1, name);
    fclose(infil[i]);
    unlink(name);  /* kill the work files */
  }
}
/*
 * Merge: merge infil[1]...infil[nfiles] onto outfil
 */
merge(nfiles, outfil)
unsigned nfiles;
int outfil;
{
  int i, inf, lbp, lp1, nf;
  lbp = 1;
  nf =0;
  for (i = 1; i <= nfiles; i++)  /* get one line from each file */
    if (fgets(&linbuf[lbp],MAXLINE, infil[i]) != NULL)
    {
      nf++;
      linptr[nf] = lbp;
      lbp += MAXLINE; /* leave room for largest line */
    }
```

160

```
   quick(nf);  /* make initial heap */
   while (nf > 0) {
     lp1 = linptr[1];
     fputs(&linbuf[lp1], outfil);
     /*putc(' \n', outfil);*/
      nf = lp1 / MAXLINE + 1; /* compute file index */
      if (fgets(&linbuf[lp1],MAXLINE,infil[inf]) == NULL)
       {
           linptr[1] = linptr[nf];
           nf--;
       }
     reheap (nf);
   }
return;
}
/*
  * Reheap: propagate linbuf [linptr[1]] to proper place in heap
  */
reheap(nf)
unsigned nf;
{
  unsigned i,j;
  for (i = 1; (i + i) <= nf; i = j)
   {
     j = i + i;
     if (j < nf) /* find smaller child */
           if (compar(linptr[j],linptr[j+1]) > 0)
       j++;
     if (compar(linptr[i], linptr[j]) <= 0)
       break;   /* Now at proper location */
     temp = linptr[i]; /* percolate */
     linptr[i] = linptr[j];
     linptr[j] = temp;
   }
  return;
}
/*
min  return the smaller of two values
*/
min(val1,val2)
unsigned int val1,val2;
{
      if (val1 < val2)
   return (val1);
   else
   return (val2);
}
/*
```

```
 * Unlink: kill the named file
 */
unlink(name)
{
  int retcod;
  strcpy(name2,"KILL ");
  strcat(name2,name);
  retcod = cmd(name2);    /* kill the file */
  return;
}


itoa(n,s)
char s[];
int n;
{
    int i, sign;
    if((sign = n) < 0)
            n = -n;
    i = 0;
    do
      {
          s[i++] = n%10 +'0';
      }
    while(( n /= 10) > 0);
    if(sign<0)
          s[i++] = '-';
    s[i] = ' \ 0';
    reverse(s);
}


reverse(s)
char s[];
{
    int c,i,j;
    for(i=0, j=strlen(s)-1; i<j; i++,j--)
      {
        c = s[i];
        s[i] = s[j];
        s[j] = c;
      }
}
```

There are a number of differences between the DeSmet version of this program and the LC version. Firstly, all of the file pointers have been changed to integers in keeping with previous programs. Secondly, some of the integers in the sort routines have been declared as register variables. These are stored in and manipulated directly in the registers of the 8088 or 8086 processor. As a result of this a significant improvement in the sort times is achieved.

Thirdly, two extra functions have been added. These are the itoa() and reverse() functions whose purpose is to convert an integer variable into a character string array. These functions are not provided as standard as in the LC compiler.

Apart from the differences in the file names, this completes the modifications needed to convert the program from one compiler to another.

Two statements have been expressed as comments in both programs. These were the putc('/n',outfil); statements. When the program was run it placed an extra linefeed after each block of text. This was not considered desirable and so was removed. The reason that they have been left in as comment lines is that some users may prefer the output of the program if these commands are left in. If this is so then it is a simple task to remove the comment delimiters.

This is the end of this chapter, but before we finish, here are two timings for the above program.

(1) for an 8 bit TRS-80 model III with a Cumana hard disk unit sorting a 32k mixed text file. Sort time = 4 min 30 secs.

(2) for an 8/16 bit Sirius (Victor) with standard 'floppy' disks sorting a 34k mixed text file. Sort time = 6 min 35 secs.

These times illustrate the fact that for any sort routine of this type the hardware is the overriding constraint on the program's efficiency. Even allowing for this, the sort times for both computers are very respectable.

Summary of Chapter 11.

(1)   Introduction to the Shell sort.

(2)   Internal version of the Shell sort.

(3)   External Sort/Merge techniques.

(4)   An external sort/merge program.

Index